BrightRED Results

Standard Grade COMPUTING STUDIES

Anne Collins

BrightRED PUBLISHING

First published in 2009 by:

Bright Red Publishing Ltd
6 Stafford Street
Edinburgh
EH3 7AU

A CIP record for this book is available from the British Library

ISBN 978-1-906736-11-8

With thanks to PDQ Digital Media, Bungay (layout) and Ivor Normand (copy-edit)

Cover design by Caleb Rutherford – eidetic

Illustrations by Armadillojam

Acknowledgements

Every effort has been made to seek all copyright holders. If any have been overlooked then Bright Red Publishing will be delighted to make the necessary arrangements.

Printed and bound in Scotland by Scotprint

Mixed Sources
Product group from well-managed forests and other controlled sources
www.fsc.org Cert no. TT-COC-002217
© 1996 Forest Stewardship Council
FSC

Contents

Introduction

This book is intended to provide candidates with a comprehensive summary of the Standard Grade course content at General and Credit levels. At the end of each topic summary, there is a selection of commonly asked exam-style questions and answers, highlighting areas of historical difficulty and offering useful tips and advice.

Statistics and information relating to the Standard Grade Computing Studies past-paper exam questions include the 2009 papers.

The course contains a significant number of abbreviations and acronyms, such as WIMP, CAD and TFT, and also many pairs of words or short phrases that candidates often mix up, such as the difference between:

- a standard letter and a standard paragraph
- serial and direct access
- data files and program files.

Therefore, the end of this book has a summary of abbreviations and acronyms and their meanings, as well as a list of pairs of words.

Look out for

The 'Arrangements in Computing Studies' are available on the SQA website and contain seven pages of detailed course content which is the source for questions set in the external paper. Do not ignore the Foundation-level arrangements, even if you are sitting the Credit and General papers, because some questions at each level incorporate content from a lower level. Under the heading 'What you need to know at **General** level' in each chapter, some Foundation-level content may be included if that content appears frequently in General or Credit-level questions.

About the course

There are three broad areas of content, the first two of which are subdivided into more specific categories:

1. Computer applications
   - general-purpose packages
   - communications
   - industrial applications/ automated systems
   - commercial data-processing
2. Computer systems
   - hardware
   - low-level machine
   - systems software
   - operating systems
3. Computer-programming.

How you will be assessed

The course will be assessed by two examinations. Candidates will either sit a Credit (grades 1 and 2) and General (grades 3 and 4) paper, or they will sit a General and Foundation (grades 5 and 6) paper.

Knowledge and Understanding (KU) and Problem-Solving (PS) are externally assessed by a written exam, and Practical Abilities (PA) is internally assessed from the folio work completed during the two-year course.

- KU – recall, describe and explain computing facts and concepts
- PS – in theoretical contexts: analyse problems; design and evaluate solutions
- PA – in practical situations: analyse problems; design, implement and evaluate practical solutions to produce a folio of project work, non-programming coursework and programming coursework.

Overall grade

Your overall grade will be the mean of your KU, PS and PA grade, weighted respectively using the ratio 1:2:2. Your best KU and PS grade over the two papers will be used.

Changes to the arrangements

The Standard Grade Computing Studies arrangements were amended in 2004 to update some of the content. Candidates were presented for the first exam relating to these new arrangements in May 2006. Although many areas of content remained largely unaltered by these amendments, candidates should be aware that there will be some differences in content if using pre-2006 past papers for revision purposes.

Look out for

Candidates sitting the Credit exam should answer the questions fully. The new layout of the Credit exam paper does **not** indicate that only General-level descriptions are all that is required.

General-purpose packages

What you need to know at **General** level ...

This particular unit is very fragmented and covers a variety of concepts, some of which are dealt with in more detail later in this book. These topics have been left out of this first chapter.

Content INCLUDED in this chapter

- select appropriate package for task
- header / footer
- HCI (human–computer interface)
- toolbar
- template / wizard
- online help
- online tutorial
- integrated packages

Content NOT INCLUDED in this chapter

but covered under Commercial data-processing (CDP), Presentation and multimedia (MM), Automated systems (AS) or Word-processing (WP)

- storage, retrieval and communication of large quantities of information (CDP)
- accurate, complete and up-to-date information (CDP)
- need for backup (CDP)
- data types (MM)
- social implications (CDP, AS)
- economic implications (CDP, AS)
- standard file formats (WP)

A **general-purpose package** is a piece of software designed so that users can enter their own data in order to carry out a variety of tasks. Depending on the selection of features provided with the package, some are more suited to processing text, while others are better at dealing with numbers or graphics.

Selecting appropriate package for task

Word-processor – for entering and editing text

Spreadsheet – mostly used to do calculations on numbers

Database – structuring data in such a way that it can be searched and sorted quickly and easily

Graphics – to create and edit pictures

Desk-top publishing – to manipulate text and graphics to produce professional-looking documents such as newspapers, magazines, posters, leaflets and flyers

Presentation and multimedia – for presenting information using a variety of media types such as numbers, text, graphics, animation, sound and video

Web-page creation – to create pages of information that can be viewed on the internet using a browser

Expert systems – attempt to act in a similar way to a human expert by drawing conclusions, making decisions and offering advice by extracting information from the user and data from the knowledge base.

Look out for

A common exam question describes a task then asks which package would be the most suitable to carry out that task.

Look out for

When asked to select the most appropriate type of package, make sure you use the generic term for the package, such as word-processor, database or spreadsheet; do **not** use specific product names such as Word, FileMaker Pro or Excel.

Header/footer – areas at the top and bottom of the page to allow the user to enter information such as chapter headings and page numbers. An **advantage** of using the header/footer feature is that the information only has to be typed **once**, and it will appear on **every** page.

HCI (human–computer interface) – the HCI is part of the **software** of an operating system or the part of a program that allows a two-way communication between the user and the computer.

Toolbar – displays a list of icons that are all linked to a particular type of task. Toolbars include: standard, formatting, picture and drawing.

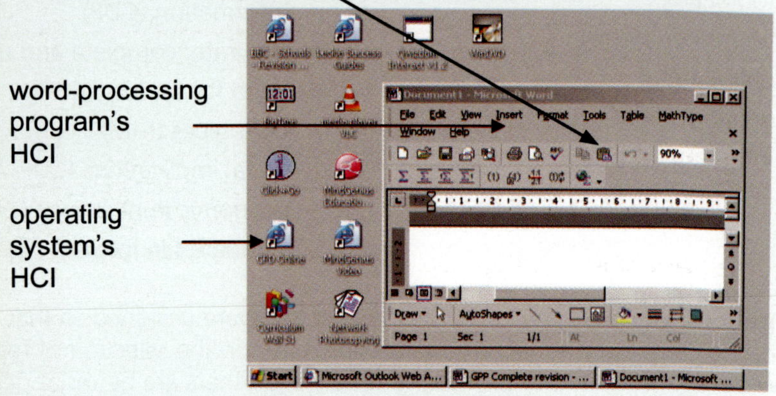

A **user-friendly HCI** is one that is easy and quick to learn and gives help when necessary.

Two examples of a user-friendly HCI are:

1. **WIMP** – Windows, Icons, Menus, Pointer
2. **GUI** – A graphical user interface uses icons to represent objects on the screen.

The word-processing program's HCI and the operating system's HCI are examples of both WIMP and GUI.

Template – a document that has been set up with placeholders for specific items of data such as text and graphics. If the same layout is required on many occasions, it is much quicker to use a template than to have to recreate the same layout each time.

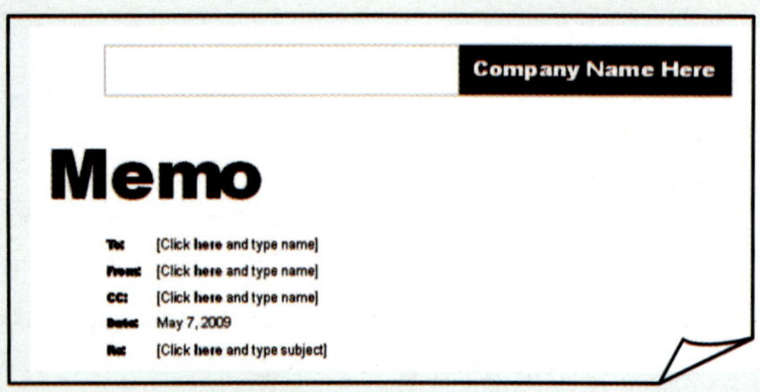

! Look out for

Human–computer interface should not be confused with a **hardware** interface, which is between a computer and a device. (See the chapter on Automated Systems.)

! Look out for

In an exam, you will **not** get any marks if you say that the M of WIMP stands for mouse, or the P for pull-down menu.

Wizard – a step-by-step dialogue that leads the user through processes such as:

- mail-merge in a word-processing package
- producing a calendar in a desk-top publishing package, or
- installing software on a computer.

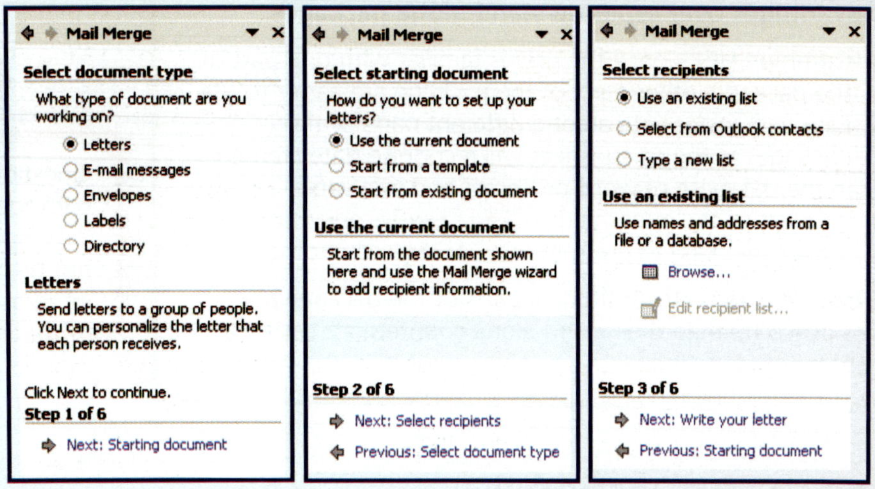

Online help is a quick look-up guide, stored on the computer, to provide help when using the package.

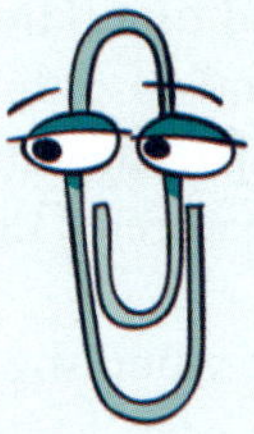

Online tutorial is a step-by-step guide, stored on the computer, to teach the user how to use the package.

Advantages of help and tutorials being **online** include:

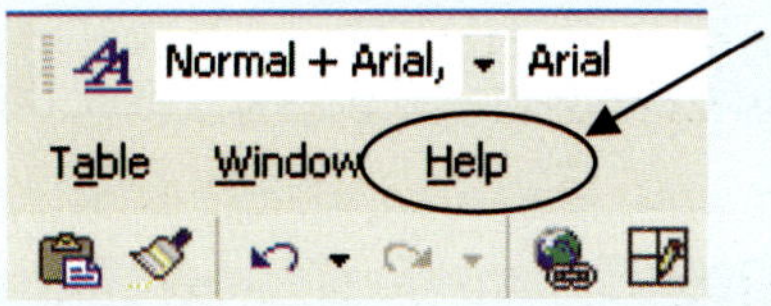

- always available, unlike a manual that might get lost
- cheaper than producing manuals
- there is one for each computer.

Look out for

A question on online help and/or online tutorial has occurred in almost every exam. See page 96, 'Exam-mark allocation'.

Look out for

Definitions for, and advantages of, templates and wizards are commonly asked in questions relating to word-processing, desk-top publishing, presentation and multimedia or web-page creation software, and often appear in the Credit paper.

Look out for

To describe the **online** part of online help or an online tutorial, a common error is assuming that 'online' means accessing the internet. Online in this context means an electronic version stored as part of the package.

Integrated packages

An integrated package is where two or more general-purpose packages are merged into a single package. The most common packages to be integrated are word-processors, databases and spreadsheets, although graphics packages are sometimes included.

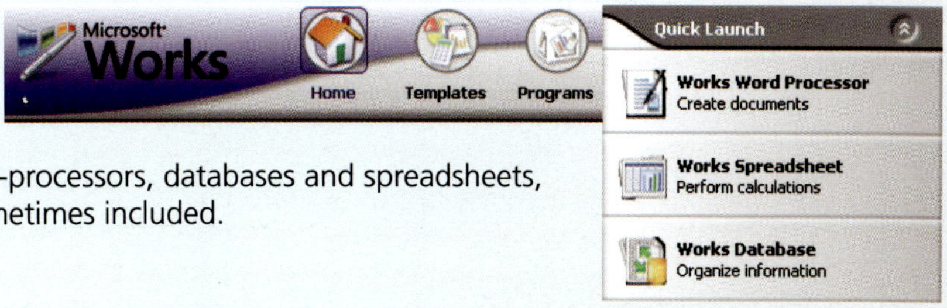

Advantages over separate stand-alone packages

- Common HCI – once the user is familiar with one part of the package, other parts of the package are easier to use.
- Easy to transfer data among different parts of the package, as the spreadsheet will recognise data created in the database or word-processor and vice versa.
- All parts of the integrated package can be open at the same time. Easy to go from one package to another.

Disadvantage – the individual parts of the package are less powerful than their stand-alone counterparts, as they contain fewer features.

Look out for

Questions relating to integrated packages have been badly answered in the past, with many candidates not being able to explain what an integrated package is.

General question 1

a) Mary decides to buy either a word-processing package or an integrated package for her computer, even though she is not a very experienced user. The sales assistant tells Mary that, once she has installed the software, she can access online help and an online tutorial.

(i) Mary chooses to buy the integrated package and is surprised at how easily she is able to install the software. Name and describe a feature of the software that made the installation easy. {PS 2}

(ii) Which online feature should she use when she first installs the software? Explain your answer. {PS 2}

(iii) Describe a situation where Mary might use the other online feature. {KU 1}

b) (i) What is an integrated package? {KU 1}

(ii) Suggest one disadvantage of choosing the integrated package over the stand-alone word-processing package. {KU 1}

a) (i) *A wizard, as it is a step-by-step dialogue that would lead Mary through the installation process.*

(ii) *Mary should use the online tutorial, as it will take her through the basic features of the package.*

(iii) *For example, Mary wants to use a drop capital at the start of her document but cannot remember how to create it, so she could use the online help facility to find out.*

b) (i) *An integrated package is where two or more general-purpose packages are merged into a single package.*

(ii) *One disadvantage is that the word-processing part of an integrated package will have fewer features than a separate word-processing package.*

What you need to know at **Credit** level ...

Keyboard shortcuts

Experienced users find it quicker to perform certain actions using keyboard shortcuts rather than using the menus and mouse, as the user may have to click on options from several menus before reaching the choice they want.

Customising the HCI

The HCI can be altered to make it more personal to the user's requirements and preferences. Examples include:

- Changing – font styles, sizes, background and menus
- How icons are viewed.

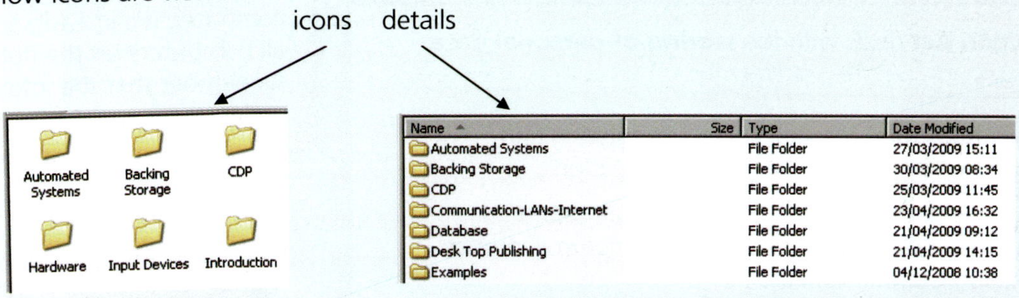

Integrated packages – static and dynamic linkage

The same data can appear in different parts of the package. The data is linked using either **static** or **dynamic** linkage.

When data is updated in one part of the package and the same data **automatically** updates in any other part of the package, **dynamic** linkage has been used. If updating data in one part of the package does **not** affect the same data anywhere else, then **static** linkage has been used.

Look out for

A question on linkage has appeared in almost every exam (see page 96).

Security and privacy

Due to the increasing quantities of personal and sensitive data being held by companies, it is vital that appropriate privacy and security measures are taken.

The following legislation has been put in place to help formalise appropriate privacy and security measures.

Look out for

There is more information on security and privacy in the chapters on communications and on commercial data-processing, including passwords, encryption and physical security.

1. Computer Misuse Act

The **Computer Misuse Act** deals with hacking and viruses.

Hacking – it is an offence to

- try to gain unauthorised access to a computer system
- gain unauthorised access to a computer system
- gain unauthorised access to a computer system and alter data – this is obviously the most serious of the hacking offences.

Writing and spreading viruses.

Look out for

Questions relating to the Computer Misuse Act may appear as part of a communications question, as it is much easier to hack into a computer on a network, especially if it is wireless. Also, once a virus is on a networked computer, it can easily spread to all computers on the network. Remember that the internet is a wide-area network!

2. Data Protection Act

The **Data Protection Act** deals with the **storing of personal data**.

Personnel involved:

Information Commissioner – responsible for regulating and enforcing the access to, and use of, personal information.

Data controller – the person responsible in an organisation for holding the data. Before storing the data, the data controller must notify the Information Commissioner.

Data subjects – the people who have data stored about them.

Data-protection principles

- Data should be lawfully processed
- Data should be accurate and kept up to date
- Data should not be kept any longer than necessary.

Rights of data subjects

- See data held about themselves (for a fee)
- Have errors corrected
- Entitled to compensation if adversely affected by the act not being adhered to.

Exceptions to the right of access

- Protection of national security
- Purpose of collecting taxes
- Crime prevention.

Look out for

There are eight principles, but you will not need to know more than three for the exam.

3. Copyright, Designs and Patents Act

The **Copyright, Designs and Patents Act** deals with a person's work being used by someone else without payment or permission.

Computing areas that might need the protection of this act are:

- copying another programmer's software without their permission
- using other people's pictures, music or video clips in multimedia presentations or on websites.

Credit question 1

a) In the example below, the data from 'Grades 1' has been used as part of Memo 1. Just before the memo is sent to the Depute Rector, the computing teacher realises that there is an error in the spreadsheet data: Susan's PS mark should have been 35, not 30. The teacher changes the mark in the 'Grades 2' spreadsheet.

(i) If the link between the spreadsheet and the word-processor is **static**, will the Depute Rector receive Memo 1 or Memo 2? {PS 1}

(ii) If the link is **dynamic**, will the Depute Rector receive Memo 1 or Memo 2? {PS 1}

b) Explain the difference between static and dynamic linkage. {KU 2}

c) Describe a situation where the user would want the linkage to be static. {KU 1}

Grades 1

	A	B	C	D
1	**S4 Prelim Grades**	**KU**	**PS**	**Overall**
2	**Susan**	30	30	**60**
3	**David**	29	32	**61**
4	**Derek**	32	34	**66**
5	**Joe**	14	12	**26**

Grades 2

	A	B	C	D
1	**S4 Prelim Grades**	**KU**	**PS**	**Overall**
2	**Susan**	30	35	**65**
3	**David**	29	32	**61**
4	**Derek**	32	34	**66**
5	**Joe**	14	12	**26**

Memo 1

Memo

To: Depute Rector

From: Computing teacher

Re: Progress of Joe

I am extremely concerned about the progress Joe is making in Computing and thought I should make you aware of this. As you can see from the spreadsheet shown below his overall S4 prelim mark is significantly worse than the rest of the class.

	A	B	C	D
1	**S4 Prelim Grades**	**KU**	**PS**	**Overall**
2	**Susan**	30	30	**60**
3	**David**	29	32	**61**
4	**Derek**	32	34	**66**
5	**Joe**	14	12	**26**

Memo 2

Memo

To: Depute Rector

From: Computing teacher

Re: Progress of Joe

I am extremely concerned about the progress Joe is making in Computing and thought I should make you aware of this. As you can see from the spreadsheet shown below his overall S4 prelim mark is significantly worse than the rest of the class.

	A	B	C	D
1	**S4 Prelim Grades**	**KU**	**PS**	**Overall**
2	**Susan**	30	35	**65**
3	**David**	29	32	**61**
4	**Derek**	32	34	**66**
5	**Joe**	14	12	**26**

a) (i) Memo 1 (ii) Memo 2

b) Dynamic linkage means that, if the same data appears in two parts of the package and it is updated in one part, it will automatically update in the other part. With static linkage, the same data in another part will not update automatically.

c) A memo containing information about each year group's monthly attendance. If a memo was sent about September's attendance, the September memo should not automatically update when October's data is entered.

Credit question 2

Match the following words, phrases or statements to one of the three acts. {KU 5}

1. Deals with the storing of personal data
2. Writing viruses
3. Attempting to gain unauthorised access to a network
4. Installing commercial software without purchasing a licence
5. Registering with the data Information Commissioner.

Data Protection Act 1, 5 Computer Misuse Act 2, 3 Copyright, Designs & Patents Act 4

! Look out for

Make sure you know the personnel, principles, rights and exceptions of the Data Protection Act, as questions relating to this act have come up every year since 2006.

Word-processing

What you need to know at General level ...

Features of a word-processor:

- standard paragraph
- search and replace
- spelling-checker
- grammar-checker
- tabulation
- table
- page breaks.

A **standard paragraph** is a saved piece of text which can be used many times.

Advantage: saves the user time in typing the paragraph and checking for errors.

Tables – advantages include:

- Makes presentation of data clearer, e.g. reading across rows
- Easier than setting out tabs
- Text can be wrapped within a table
- Easy to insert rows and columns.

The **search-and-replace** facility allows the user to search for a particular string of characters in a document and replace it by another. For example, search for 'fitness' and replace by 'health'.

A **spell-checker** works by

- checking each word in the document against those in its dictionary
- highlighting any word not in its dictionary
- suggesting, where possible, alternative words.

To prevent a **spell-checker** from identifying a correct word as incorrect, you can **either** add the word to the dictionary **or** select 'ignore all' (it is not acceptable to select 'ignore' on its own).

A **grammar-checker** works by

- checking words, phrases and sentences against a set of rules
- highlighting words or sentences that it thinks have a grammatical error
- suggesting alternative words or phrases.

Look out for

When being asked 'What is a standard **paragraph**?', a common mistake made by candidates in previous exams has been to describe a standard **letter** instead of a standard **paragraph**.

Fitness for Fun
Slim Lane
SL8 1FF

Dear Miss Watson

Thank you very much for the interest you have shown in our fitness club. Below is the information you have requested:

Open Days
We hold an open day on the first and third Saturday of every month from 10am to 4pm. No appointment required, just come along and one of our fitness instructors will show you around.

Club Fees

Type of member	Days per week	Cost per week
Junior (Under 5's free)	7 days a week	£25
Adult	7 days a week	£50
Adult	Week days only	£40

We look forward to hearing from you in the near future.

Yours Sincerely
Suzie Skip

Look out for

The use of tables and explaining their advantages over, say, tabs is a topic that has not been answered well in previous exams.

Tabulation allows the user to align text and/or numbers in columns set by tab stops on the ruler.

A **page break** is used to force the word-processor to start a new page.

In this example, a page break (-----------) could be inserted before the last line at the bottom of the first page to keep the two parts of the paragraph together.

Look out for

Few candidates were able to identify a page break when it last appeared in an exam.

General question

a) The receptionist at Fitness for Fun is about to send out a letter to Miss Wilson when she realises it should have been Miss Watson. Her name has been used several times throughout the letter. What could be done to correct this in a single operation? {PS 2}

b) Before sending out any letter, the receptionist uses both the spell-checker and the grammar-checker. Give an example of a mistake that might be highlighted by each of these tools. {KU 2}

c) Every week, the receptionist uses the table feature of her word-processor to type up a timetable of all the classes that are on offer. Give two reasons for using a table. {PS 2}

a) *There are three common answers to this question:*
Answer 1 – Use the search-and-replace facility.
Answer 2 – Use the search-and-replace facility to search for the incorrect word and replace it by the correct word.
Answer 3 – Use the search-and-replace facility to search for 'Wilson' and replace it by 'Watson'.
Only answer 3 will get full marks. (The marks are for problem-solving, so the answer must include information from the given scenario.)

b) *Spell-checker – an incorrectly spelt word (e.g. jym instead of gym) or a proper name (e.g. Cortachy) that is not in the dictionary.*
Grammar-checker – using the wrong spelling of a word (to/two/too) or wrong word or tense (I were late) or incorrect punctuation (missing full stop, or no capital at the start of the sentence).

c) *1. Easy to insert a row or column if an additional class has to be added.*
2. A table makes the presentation of data clearer, thus making it easier for clients to find the classes they are looking for.

Look out for

In part b), check the wording in the question, as you may be asked for a description of how each tool works rather than giving an actual example.

Look out for

Make sure you know the difference between a 'standard paragraph' and a 'standard letter'.

What you need to know at **Credit** level ...

Features of a word-processor:

- standard letter
- mail-merge
- create template
- edit scanned text from OCR
- standard file formats.

> Fitness for Fun
> Slim Lane
> SL8 1FF
>
> Dear
>
> As a valued customer we would like to invite you to our summer barbeque on 25th June. Enclosed are complementary tickets for you and four guests. As a member you are also entitled to % discount on all refreshments.
>
> Hope to see you there.
>
> From all the staff at Fitness for Fun.

Standard letter

A word-processed letter with the same general content for each person, with spaces left for personal details such as name and address, which will be different for each person.

Mail-merge

The **two applications** in mail-merge are:

1. a word-processor (to create the letter) and
2. a database (to store personal details).

Mail-merge is the process of merging personal details from the database into the standard letter.

Last Name	First Name	Title	Category	Discount
Watson	Linda	Mrs	Gold	30
Brown	James	Mr	Bronze	10
Gillies	Fiona	Dr	Gold	30
Asher	Susan	Miss	Silver	20

> Fitness for Fun
> Slim Lane
> SL8 1FF
>
> Dear **<<Title>>** **<<Last Name>>**
>
> As a valued customer we would like to invite you to our summer barbeque on 25th June. Enclosed are complimentary tickets for you and four guests. As a **<<Category>>** member you are also entitled to **<<Discount>>** % discount on all refreshments.
>
> Hope to see you there.
>
> From all the staff at Fitness for Fun.

The steps involved

- Type the letter using a word-processing package, with placeholders for personal details
- Create or load the database containing the personal details
- Insert the appropriate field names from the database into the standard letter
- If necessary, filter the database for the required records
- Print-merge the letters
- Post the letters (known as 'mailshot').

Create template

A template determines the basic structure of a document, with placeholders for text and graphics, and contains settings such as fonts, special formatting and styles.

This speeds up the creation of the document, as much of the layout has already been done.

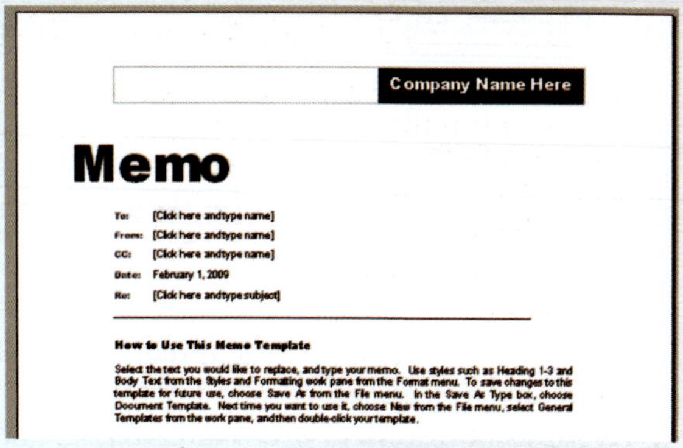

Company Name Here

Memo

To: [Click here andtype name]
From: [Click here andtype name]
CC: [Click here andtype name]
Date: February 1, 2009
Re: [Click here andtype subject]

How to Use This Memo Template

Select the text you would like to replace, and type your memo. Use styles such as Heading 1-3 and Body Text from the Styles and Formatting work pane from the Format menu. To save changes to this template for future use, choose Save As from the File menu. In the Save As Type box, choose Document Template. Next time you want to use it, choose New from the File menu, select General Templates from the work pane, andthen double-click yourtemplate.

Optical character recognition (OCR)

A scanner with optical character recognition software can be used to scan in words from a paper document and convert them into a new word-processed document which can be edited.

If you only have a paper copy of the text, scanning is much faster than entering the text using a keyboard – but, once scanned, the text may have to be edited, as errors can occur during the conversion process. For example, an 'i' in the original document may be scanned as a capital 'I'.

Standard file formats

A standard file format is a way of storing data so that it can be recognised by different application packages. Standard file formats used in word-processing include:

ASCII (or TXT) – only stores the words, spaces and punctuation

RTF (Rich Text Format) – stores the words, spaces and punctuation as well as formatting such as styles, fonts and sizes.

Look out for

Make sure you can give an advantage of a standard file format, as this has been poorly answered in the past.

Look out for

Make sure you know what RTF stands for.

Credit question 1

a) Sarah, a fourth-year pupil at ABC High, has been word-processing her English folio work at home, but her printer has run out of ink, and the school uses different word-processing software. What can she do so that she is able to print out her work using a school printer? {PS 2}

b) (i) Sarah has a printout of a piece of folio work that she did in third year. Her teacher has suggested some improvements, but she has accidentally deleted the document. What could she do to save retyping her work? (PS 1}

(ii) Sarah used both the spell-checker and grammar-checker on the original paper document. Can she assume that the new word-processed document will still have no errors? Explain your answer. {KU 1}

a) Save her document using a common file format such as Rich Text Format (RTF), as this is recognised by all word-processing programs and retains formatting information such as fonts and indentation.

b) (i) Use a scanner that has Optical Character Recognition software.

(ii) No, the document could have errors because the scanning process does not always give perfect results.

Credit question 2

At the start of the school session, sixth-year pupils at ABC High School are given the opportunity to go on an Outward Bound activities week. The school secretary sends out standard letters to all their parents with information about the week.

a) What is a standard letter? {KU 2}

b) A word-processor was used to create the standard letter. What other type of package is required to produce personalised letters? {KU 1}

c) What can be done so that standard letters do not go to parents of all pupils? {PS 1}

d) A template can be used to speed up the creation of standard letters.
   (i) What is a template? {KU 1}
   (ii) State one advantage of using a template. {KU 1}

Look out for

A common, **incorrect** answer to part b) of this question is mail-merge. Mail-merge is **not** an application package; it is the **process** of inserting personal data into a standard letter.

a) The main points when describing a standard letter are:
   1. A letter with the same general content
   2. To be sent to many people
   3. With space to insert personalised details such as name and address.

b) A database.

c) Filter the database by searching the year field 'equal to' or 'contains' 6.

d) (i) A template is a ready-made document with structure in place for text and possibly graphics.
   (ii) Quicker to create document, and user does not need to design layout.

Look out for

Make sure you know:

1. the steps required in the process of setting up a mail-merge, AND
2. that you can give a clear definition of a standard letter, as there has been a question associated with standard letters and/or mail-merge in the Credit paper **every** year.

Spreadsheets

What you need to know at General level ...

A spreadsheet is a general-purpose package that helps the user to present rows and columns of numerical data with features that include:

- complex formulae
- functions – sum, average, max and min
- replication
- alteration of cell format and attributes
- cell protection.

Complex formulae

The cell D3 contains the formula =C3–B3. This is an example of a simple formula, as it only uses one operator (operators include + – * /). Complex formulae are more complicated because they use more than one operator. The profit column in E shows examples of complex formulae.

When you use complex formulae in a spreadsheet, the rules for the order in which calculations are carried out are the same as in mathematics or on a calculator:

- brackets
- powers
- multiplication and division
- adding and subtracting.

	A	B	C	D	E
1	Item	Buying	Selling	Amount	Profit
2		Price	Price	Sold	in £'s
3	Bread	36	47	106	=((C3-B3)*D3)/100
4	Rolls	9	12	225	=((C4-B4)*D4)/100
5	Milk	30	35	90	=((C5-B5)*D5)/100
6	Butter	56	62	50	=((C6-B6)*D6)/100

Functions: Sum | Average | Maximum | Minimum

Functions in a spreadsheet provide valuable shortcuts to formula creation. Four useful functions are exemplified in cells B8 to B11.

SUM function
B8 **=SUM(B2:B6)** – totals all the numbers contained in the range of cells from B2 to B6.

AVERAGE function
B9 **=AVERAGE(B2:B6)** – calculates the average of the numbers contained in the range of cells from B2 to B6.

MAX function
B10 **=MAX(B2:B6)** – finds the largest number contained in the range of cells from B2 to B6.

MIN function
B11 **=MIN(B2:B6)** – finds the smallest number contained in the range of cells from B2 to B6.

	A	B
1	**Name**	**Height**
2	Susan	150
3	John	170
4	David	165
5	Gordon	175
6	Sarah	155
7		
8	**Total**	815
9	**Average**	163
10	**Tallest**	175
11	**Smallest**	150

Look out for

Every year, there is a spreadsheet question in both the General and Credit papers.

Replication

Replication means copying down or across into one or more cells. This is especially useful if you want to use the same formula in several rows or columns. It is much faster than typing the formulae individually – and, as long as the original formula is correct, it reduces the chance of error.

	A	B
1	1	=A1*12
2	2	↓
3	3	↓
4	4	↓
5	5	↓
6		

Alteration of cell format and attributes

Data that has been typed in can have its appearance altered in a number of different ways. Formatting cells in this way is referred to as altering cells' attributes. Examples include:

- bold / underline / italics
- right-justified
- currency and 2 decimal places.

Cell protection

Spreadsheet packages allow you to protect or lock the contents of a cell or cells that you do not want to be altered by accident. This is especially useful if someone else is going to use the spreadsheet.

General question

Gary, one of the house captains, designed a spreadsheet to record the outcome of a recent inter-house hockey tournament. Each team was awarded 4 points for a win and 2 points for a draw. In addition, each point earned the team's house £10.

	A	B	C	D	E	F
1	**Team**	**Won**	**Drawn**	**Lost**	**Points**	**Payout**
2	A	3	2	1	16	160
3	B	2	3	1	14	140
4	C	1	2	3	8	80
5	D	1	3	2	10	100
6						
7				**Biggest Payout**		£160.00
8				**Average Payout**		£120.00

a) A complex formula has been used in cell E2. Suggest an appropriate formula. {PS 2}

b) The formula to calculate the payout was only entered once in cell F2 then replicated into cells F3 to F5. Describe how this formula was replicated. {PS 2}

c) Functions have been used in cells F7 and F8. Write down suitable functions. {PS 4}

d) What attribute has been applied to the numbers in cells F7 and F8? {PS 1}

e) Gary wants to stop other pupils from altering the formulae when they are entering the tournament results. Explain what feature he must use to stop this happening. {KU 1}

f) State one way in which cell B1 has been formatted. {PS 1}

a) =(B2*4)+(C2*2)

b) Highlight cell F2, then drag the bottom right-hand corner of the cell down into cells F3 to F5.

c) F7 =MAX(F2:F5) (2 marks), F8 =AVERAGE(F2:F5)

d) Currency

e) Use cell protection / lock the cells

f) Bold, right-justified.

Look out for

The spreadsheet questions are very similar from one year to the next; it is just the scenario that changes.

Look out for

You can double-check some of your answers by putting the numbers used in the spreadsheet into any function or formula you suggest to make sure that the answers match.

What you need to know at **Credit** level ...

- relative referencing
- absolute referencing
- formulae involving conditions (IF(..))
- fully labelled charting.

Look out for

A question on relative and/or absolute referencing has occurred in every paper since 2006. This is usually a problem-solving question, and it is therefore vital that you understand and can explain both types of referencing. If you find it difficult to explain yourself, clarify your answer with an example.

Relative referencing

When replicating a formula down several rows or across several columns, the spreadsheet automatically alters the row or column in the copied formula relative to where it is being copied from.

In the 'House Points' example, if you enter the formula =B2+C2 into cell D2 and replicate it down into rows 3 and 4, the spreadsheet would automatically alter the formula to:

=B**3**+C**3** in row **3** and
=B**4**+C**4** in row **4**.

House Points – showing values

	A	B	C	D
1	**House Points**	Term 1/2	Term 3/4	Total
2	Esk	300	250	550
3	Clova	425	225	650
4	Lindores	375	200	575
5				
6	Most Points	425	250	650

Similarly, if you enter the function =MAX(B2:B4) into cell B6 and replicate it across into columns C and D, the spreadsheet would automatically alter the function to:

=MAX(**C**2:**C**4) in column **C** and
=MAX(**D**2:**D**4) in column **D**.

House Points – showing formula

	A	B	C	D
1	**House Points**	Term 1/2	Term 3/4	Total
2	Esk	300	250	=B2+C2
3	Clova	425	225	=B3+C3
4	Lindores	375	200	=B4+C4
5				
6	Most Points	=MAX(B2:B4)	=MAX(C2:C4)	=MAX(D2:D4)

This is known as **relative referencing**.

Look out for

Usually, some General-level questions are asked in the Credit exam because the only Credit-level features are: relative and absolute referencing; the IF function; and fully labelled charting. The most common General-level questions asked in the Credit paper are: suggesting suitable formulae; replication; and cell attributes.

Absolute referencing

There are occasions where the user does not want all or part of the formula to change during replication.

For example, if the formula in cell E2 used only relative referencing, then the formula would be =D2*B6. When this formula was replicated into cell E3, it would read =D3*B7. As there is no data in cell B7, this formula would display the wrong answer. The cell B6 has to have an absolute reference so that it stays as cell B6, no matter where it is being replicated to.

This is done by putting a $ sign in front of each part of the cell reference: $B$6.

	A	B	C	D	E
1	Café **Weekend Staff**	Saturday	Sunday	Total Hours Worked	Wages Due
2	Emily	5	7	12	£60.00
3	James	6	0	6	£30.00
4	Karen	7	4	11	£55.00
5					
6	Wages per hour	£5.00			
7					

	A	B	C	D	E
1	Café **Weekend Staff**	Saturday	Sunday	Total Hours Worked	Wages Due
2	Emily	5	7	=B2+C2	=D2*$B$6
3	James	6	0	=B3+C3	=D3*$B$6
4	Karen	7	4	=B4+C4	=D4*$B$6
5					
6	Wages per hour	5			
7					

The formulae in column E contain both a relative **and** an absolute reference.

=D2*$B$6

Formulae involving conditions (IF(..))

The IF statement makes a decision based on the condition and the contents of any cells it references.

	A	B	C
1	**Exams**	**Mark**	**Result**
2	Joe	52	=IF(B2>=50,"Pass","Fail")
3	Alison	45	=IF(B3>=50,"Pass","Fail")
4	Helen	69	=IF(B4>=50,"Pass","Fail")

	A	B	C
1	**Exams**	**Mark**	**Result**
2	Joe	52	Pass
3	Alison	45	Fail
4	Helen	69	Pass

=IF(condition, value if true, value if false)

The 'value if true' and 'value if false' can be text, values, cells or formulae. Other examples include:

=IF(D2 > 50, 1, 0)

=IF(A1 <= 10, B1, C1)

=IF(F6 = 21, B6*C6, B6)

Look out for

Make sure you understand the IF condition, as it is a problem-solving question and has appeared in every paper since 2006.

Look out for

If you are displaying text in an IF condition, the text must be in quotation marks. There should be no quotation marks otherwise.

Charting

The charting facility within a spreadsheet application allows the user to display numerical data in a way that is quick and easy to read.

The 'House Points' spreadsheet includes data about the total points for each house. At a glance, it is not obvious which house has the most points; but the same data displayed as a chart immediately shows Clova to have the most points.

	A	B	C	D
1	**House Points**	Term 1/2	Term 3/4	Total
2	Esk	300	250	550
3	Clova	425	225	650
4	Lindores	375	200	575
5				
6	Most Points	425	250	650

Line graph

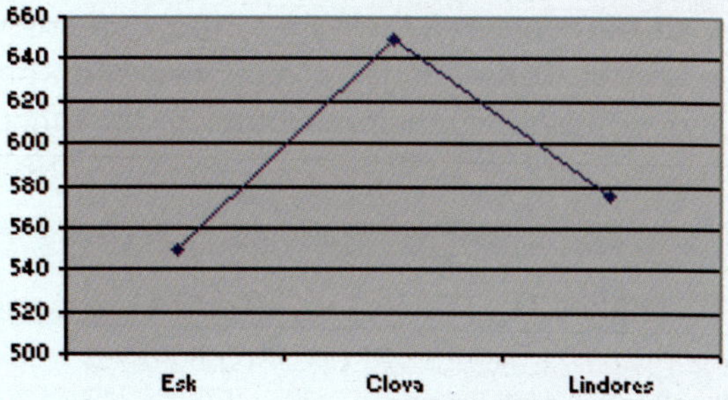

Column chart

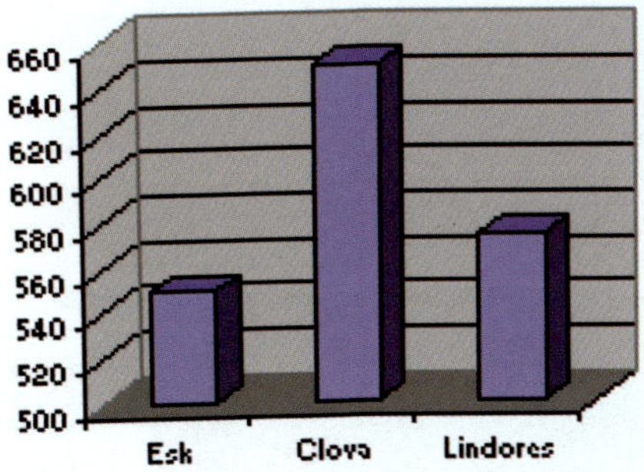

Bar chart

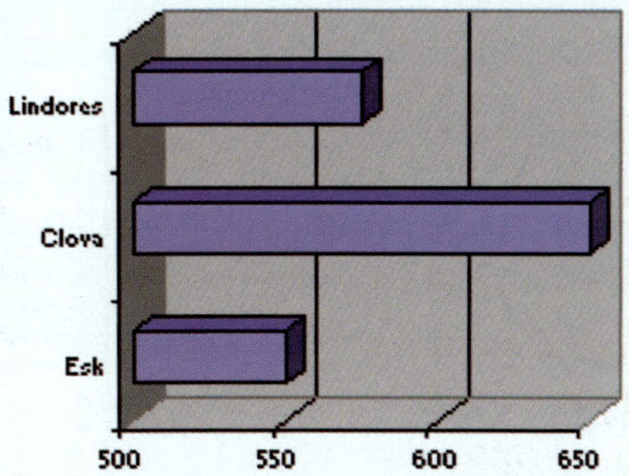

Pie chart

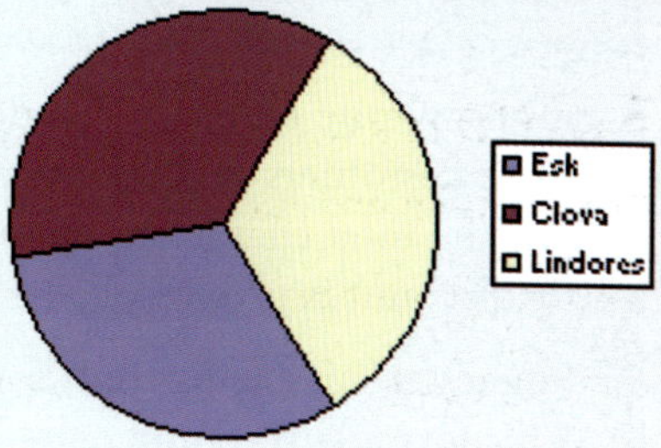

Fully labelled charting

The chart wizard facility takes the user through the steps necessary to create a fully labelled chart. This means that, as well as a label for each item in the chart, the user can give the chart a title and an x-axis category and a y-axis value.

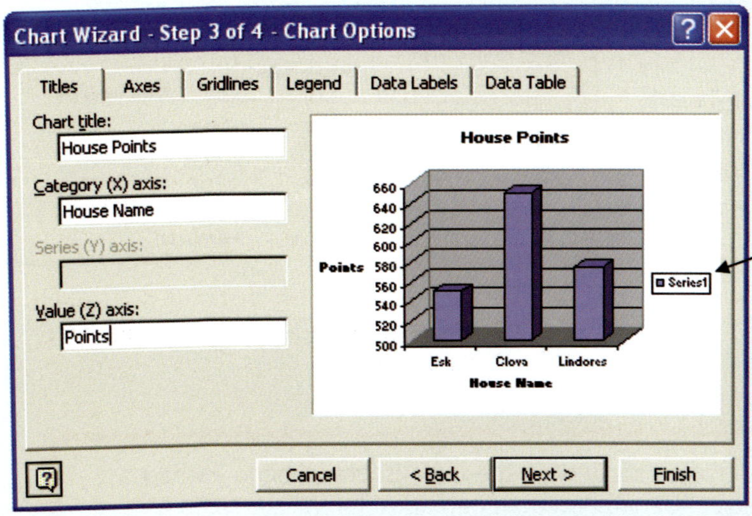

It is also possible to name the chart series.

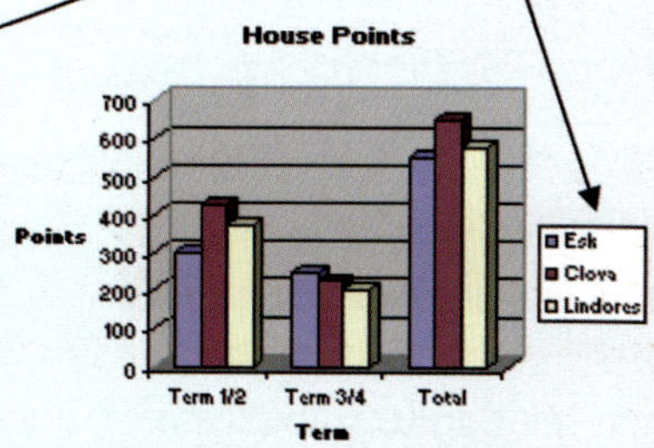

Credit question 1

	A	B	C	D	E	F	G
1	Weight Loss (in lbs)	Week 1	Week 2	Week 3	Week 4	Total Loss	Target Reached?
2	Sally	2	2	2	2	8	Yes
3	Jake	2	1	2	1	6	No
4	Avril	1	0.5	1	0.5	3	No
5	Penny	3	3	3	1	10	Yes
6							
7	Target Monthly Loss	8					

Shape Up Weight Loss Club recommends a monthly weight loss of 8 lb.

a) State the formula that will be used to calculate Sally's total loss in cell F2. {PS 1}

b) The formula in cell F2 is copied into cells F3 to F5. State the type of referencing used. Explain your answer. {PS 2}

c) State another word for 'copied' when referring to spreadsheets. {KU 1}

d) Cell G2 contains a function to show whether or not people have reached their target. If the Total Loss is greater than or equal to the Target Monthly Loss, then they have reached their target. Part of the function is shown below. Complete the function. {PS 2}

=______(F2>=$B$7,____________,"No")

a) =SUM(B2:E2)

b) Relative referencing. The cell references will change when copied from one cell to another.

c) Replicated/replication

d) =IF(F2>=$B$7,"Yes","No")

Credit question 2

	A	B	C	D
1	Mobile Phone Charges			
2		Texts Sent	Weekly charge (pence)	Weekly charge (£s)
3				
4	Week 1	150	1500	£15.00
5	Week 2	200	2000	£20.00
6	Week 3	400	4000	£40.00
7	Week 4	125	1250	£12.50
8				
9	Cost per text	10		
10			Total Charge	£87.50
11			Discount	£8.75

A mobile-phone company has designed a spreadsheet to calculate customers' monthly text bills. All texts cost 10p each. If the total charge for the month is £50 or more, a 10% discount is given.

a) Suggest a suitable formula for cell C4. {PS 2}

b) This formula was only entered once in cell C4. It has been replicated from C4 into cells C5 to C7. What is meant by replication? {KU 1}

c) State the type of referencing used. Explain your answer. {PS 2}

d) A discount of 10% is given to a total charge of £50 or more; otherwise, a No Discount message is displayed. Suggest a suitable function for cell D11. {PS 3}

a) =B4*$B$9

b) The formula has been copied.

c) Relative referencing has been used so that the cell reference for B4 will change as it moves down the rows, and absolute referencing has been used for $B$9 so it remains the same no matter where it is copied to.

d) =IF(D10>=50,D10*10%,"No Discount")

	A	B	C	D
1	Mobile Phone Charges			
2		Texts Sent	Weekly charge (pence)	Weekly charge (£s)
3				
4	Week 1	150	=B4*$B$9	=C4/100
5	Week 2	200	=B5*$B$9	=C5/100
6	Week 3	400	=B6*$B$9	=C6/100
7	Week 4	125	=B7*$B$9	=C7/100
8				
9	Cost per text	10		
10			Total Charge	=SUM(D4:D7)
11			Discount	=IF(D10>=50,D10*10%,"No Discount")
12				

Look out for

A question relating to static/dynamic linkage is often included in the spreadsheet scenario – where a chart is included in a word-processed memo (see 'General-purpose packages' for an example).

Databases

What you need to know at General level ...

Features of a database:

- alter record format
- field types
- search on more than one field
- sort on more than one field
- complex search using the CD-ROM or internet (see Chapter 2: Communications).

A database is a collection of data that is structured in such a way that it can be updated, searched and sorted quickly and easily.

Look out for

Make sure you do not muddle up the terminologies for databases and spreadsheets. Databases refer to field names, records and fields, whereas spreadsheets refer to columns, rows and cells.

Name	Height	DOB	Feed Time	Colour	Stable Block
Tilona	158	24/04/2001	06:30	Bay	3
Treble Trix	144	15/03/1996	07:00	Grey	2
Star	138	12/05/1998	06:45	Chestnut	1
White Lady	128	17/04/2003	06:45	Grey	1
Copper	158	04/04/2000	06:45	Chestnut	1
High Jinx	148	21/02/1998	06:30	Black	3
Paddy	152	11/05/2006	07:00	Dun	2
Cracker	128	02/02/1997	06:30	Grey	3
Charlie	138	19/03/2002	06:30	Grey	3

A **record** is all the data about one entry.

A **field** is a single piece of data. A **data file** is a collection of related records.

List and record format

In the exam questions, the database may be shown in list format (several records shown in one list) or in record format (one record of data).

List format

	Name	Height	DOB	Feed Time	Colour	Stable Block
1	Tilona	158	24/04/2001	06:30	Bay	3
2	Treble Trix	144	15/03/1996	07:00	Grey	2
3	Star	138	12/05/1998	06:45	Chestnut	1
4	White Lady	128	17/04/2003	06:45	Grey	1
5	Copper	158	04/04/2000	06:45	Chestnut	1
6	High Jinx	148	21/02/1998	06:30	Black	3
7	Paddy	152	11/05/2006	07:00	Dun	2
8	Cracker	128	02/02/1997	06:30	Grey	3
9	Charlie	138	19/03/2002	06:30	Grey	3

Record format

Name: Tilona
Height: 158
DOB: 24/04/2001
Feed Time: 06:30
Colour: Bay
Stable Block: 3

Look out for

Many different organisations store our personal data in electronic databases. Therefore, questions relating to

- the Data Protection Act (security and privacy of personal data) and
- the Computer Misuse Act (unauthorised access to data and virus distribution)

are often linked to database exam questions.

Alter record format

This includes adding or deleting a field, changing the field type or changing the size of a field.

	Name	Height	DOB	Feed Time	Colour	Stable Block
1	Tilona	158	24/04/2001	06:30	Bay	3
2	Treble Trix	144	15/03/1996	07:00	Grey	2
3	Star	138	12/05/1998	06:45	Chestnut	1
4	White Lady	128	17/04/2003	06:45	Grey	1

	Name	Height	Colour	Stable
1	Tilona	158	Bay	3
2	Treble Trix	144	Grey	2
3	Star	138	Chestnut	1
4	White Lady	128	Grey	1

Field types - numeric, text, graphic, date and time.

Name: Tilona **(text)**
Height: 158 **(numeric)**
DOB: 24/04/2001 **(date)**
Feed Time: 06:30 **(time)**
Photo: **(graphic)**

Name: Tilona
Height: 158
DOB: 24/04/2001
Feed Time: 06:30
Colour: Bay
Stable Block: 3

Look out for

Field types are associated with databases whereas **data types** are associated with multimedia (text, graphics, sound, animation and video).

Look out for

The words 'filter' or 'query' are sometimes used instead of the word 'search'.

Look out for

When stating what you are searching for, use the exact data in the sample database, not the data in the question – in this example, use 07:00, NOT 7am.

Search on one field (simple search)

To describe a search, keep to a set of succinct rules:

1. Start with the word 'search'
2. State the name of the field to be searched
3. Use an appropriate condition such as equal to, greater than, contains …
4. State the word or phrase you are looking for (compare to).

Question 1 – Produce a list of the horses that are fed at 7am.

Filter definition

Field name	Comparison	Compare To
Feed Time	is equal to	07:00

Answer 1 – Search 'Feed Time' field equal to 07:00.

Search on more than one field (complex search)

To describe a search on more than one field, you would follow the rules above twice, with an AND or an OR in between, depending on whether or not both sets of conditions need to be met.

Question 2 – Produce a list of all the grey horses in stable block 3.

Filter definition

	Field name	Comparison	Compare To
	Colour	is equal to	Grey
and	Stable Block	is equal to	3

Answer 2 – Search 'Colour' field equal to grey AND search 'Stable Block' field equal to 3.

Sort on one field

Sorting on **a text** field puts items in alphabetical order from A to Z or Z to A.

Sorting on a **numeric** field puts numbers in order from smallest to biggest OR from biggest to smallest.

To describe a sort, again keep to a succinct set of rules:

1. Start with the word 'Sort'
2. State the name of the field to be sorted
3. State whether the sort is ascending (A–Z or 0–9) or descending (Z–A or 9–0).

Look out for

In previous years, describing a complex sort has proved difficult for candidates.

Question 1 – Describe how you would sort this database so that the pupils are listed in order of their mark as shown.

	Surname	Forename	Class	Sex	Mark
1	Smith	Lee	2C	M	87
2	Aitken	Andrew	2A	M	75
3	Clark	Sarah	2B	F	72
4	Jones	Grant	2B	M	65
5	Black	Fiona	2A	F	64
6	Milne	Karen	2C	F	54
7	Henderson	Kevin	2B	M	43
8	Watson	James	2A	M	32
9	McDade	Claire	2C	F	21

Answer 1 – Sort 'Mark' field descending.

Sorting on more than one field

Question 2 – Describe how this database has been sorted.

	Surname	Forename	Class	Sex	Mark
1	Aitken	Andrew	2A	M	75
2	Black	Fiona	2A	F	64
3	Watson	James	2A	M	32
4	Clark	Sarah	2B	F	72
5	Henderson	Kevin	2B	M	43
6	Jones	Grant	2B	M	65
7	McDade	Claire	2C	F	21
8	Milne	Karen	2C	F	54
9	Smith	Lee	2C	M	87

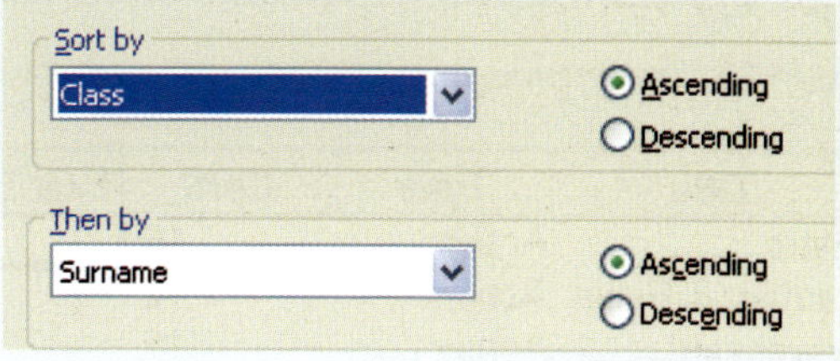

Answer 2 – It has been sorted by 'Class' field ascending, then by 'Surname' field ascending.

Look out for

A mistake often made by pupils is finding a sort on one field and not remembering to look for a second field that has been sorted.

Look out for

If you are not sure if a search or sort is required: **Search** is used when you know what you are looking for; **Sort** is used to put items into alphabetic order or to find the biggest, smallest, highest, lowest, oldest or youngest, and so on.

This is an extract from a video database held by a video and DVD hire shop. The shop has decided to sell these videos, as the films are old and most people want to hire DVDs.

Videos Credit Exemplar.wdb

	Title	Type	Cert.	Last Borrowed	No. times	Hire price
1	Scream	Horror	18	X	5	£3.50
2	The Jerk	Comedy	15	12/03/00	3	£0.50
3	Batman & Robin	Action	12	X	10	£2.50
4	Romeo & Juliet	Romance	15	18/04/00	7	£3.50
5	Braveheart	Action	15	19/05/00	8	£2.50
6	Loch Ness	Family	PG	03/02/00	15	£2.00
7	Bird Cage	Comedy	12	12/03/99	12	£2.50
8	Metro	Action	15	04/09/99	13	£1.50
9	Freddie Kruger	Horror	18	15/01/00	6	£1.50
10	Ace Ventura	Comedy	12	10/02/00	12	£1.00
11	Jerry McGuire	Romance	15	24/04/00	2	£3.00
12	Dirty Dancing	Romance	15	X	14	£2.00
13	Dennis	Family	PG	30/01/00	5	£1.50

a) Identify the field types for 'Title', 'No. times' and 'Last Borrowed'. {PS 3}

b) The data file needs to be changed to include the year the film was made. Explain how this could be done. {KU 1}

c) To advertise the different genres for sale, the owner wants a list of all the comedy films suitable for 12-year-olds. Describe how he could obtain this information. {PS 3}

d) How would you find all the films that cost £2.50 to hire and have been borrowed more than five times? {PS 3}

e) Describe how you could find the most expensive action film. {PS 3}

f) Explain what has happened to produce the data file in the order shown below. {PS 2}

g) Explain what the 'X' in some of the date fields might signify. {PS 2}

Title	Type	Cert.	Last Borrowed	No. times	Hire price
Metro	Action	15	04/09/99	13	£1.50
Batman & Robin	Action	12	X	10	£2.50
Braveheart	Action	15	19/05/00	8	£2.50
Bird Cage	Comedy	12	12/03/99	12	£2.50
Ace Ventura	Comedy	12	10/02/00	12	£1.00
The Jerk	Comedy	15	12/03/00	3	£0.50
Loch Ness	Family	PG	03/02/00	15	£2.00
Dennis	Family	PG	30/01/00	5	£1.50
Freddie Kruger	Horror	18	15/01/00	6	£1.50
Scream	Horror	18	X	5	£3.50
Dirty Dancing	Romance	15	X	14	£2.00
Romeo & Juliet	Romance	15	18/04/00	7	£3.50
Jerry McGuire	Romance	15	24/04/00	2	£3.00

a) 'Title': text, 'No. times': numeric, 'Last Borrowed': date.
b) Adding a new field – field name: 'Year', field type: numeric.
c) Search 'Type' field equal to 'Comedy' AND search 'Cert.' field equal to '12'.
d) Search 'Hire price' field = 2.5 AND search 'No. times' field greater than 5.
e) Search 'Type' field equal to 'Action', then sort 'Hire price' field descending.
f) Sort 'Type' field ascending, then sort 'No. times' field descending.
g) That the film is out on loan or has never been returned.

What you need to know at **Credit** level ...

Computed (or calculated) field

A computed field will carry out a calculation on one or more fields in the database. A calculated field is similar to a **formula** in a spreadsheet.

In the horse example, a calculated field could be added to calculate the height of the horse in inches. The calculated field would contain the calculation **= Height / 2.54**

Use of keywords

When searching a database, a CD-ROM or the internet, the user does not know exactly what data is being stored. Let's suppose the user is looking for a book on horses. By searching using the **keyword** 'horse', books with titles such as *Horses and Ponies, Training the Young Horse* and *The Horse Encyclopedia* would all be displayed, even though the user did not know the title of any of the books.

! Look out for

See also 'Search engine with simple and complex search' in the 'internet' topic for more information on keywords.

! Look out for

Often, General-level questions such as 'Search or sort on two fields' are asked in the Credit paper due to the lack of content for databases at Credit level.

Credit question

The following sample record is taken from a school database.

Field Name	Sample Data	Validation Check
Name	Fiona Black	
Class	2A	
Age	14	
Sex	F	M or F
House	Esk	
Numeracy Mark	80	>= 0 and <=100
Literacy Mark	60	>= 0 and <=100
Health Improvement Mark	30	>= 0 and <= 50

a) A computed field could be added to calculate the total of the three marks.
   (i) Explain the term 'computed field'. {KU 1}
   (ii) What data would the computed field contain? {PS 2}

b) What would have to be done to sort the database alphabetically by surname? {PS 1}

c) Name the type of validation check used for the three marks (see Chapter 4 – CDP). {PS 1}

d) (i) Which act states that the data must be kept secure? {KU 1}
   (ii) What would the school have to do before storing the data? {KU 1}

a) (i) A computed field carries out a calculation using one or more fields in the database.
(ii) = Numeracy Mark + Literacy Mark + Health Improvement Mark

b) Create another field so that there is a forename and a surname field.

c) A range check

d) (i) Data Protection Act
(ii) Data controller has to register with the Information Commissioner.

Look out for

In more recent papers, a validation check is regularly being linked to database questions rather than CDP questions – this could also be asked at General level.

Graphics

What you need to know at **General** level ...

Graphics package

A graphics package allows the user to create and edit pictures.

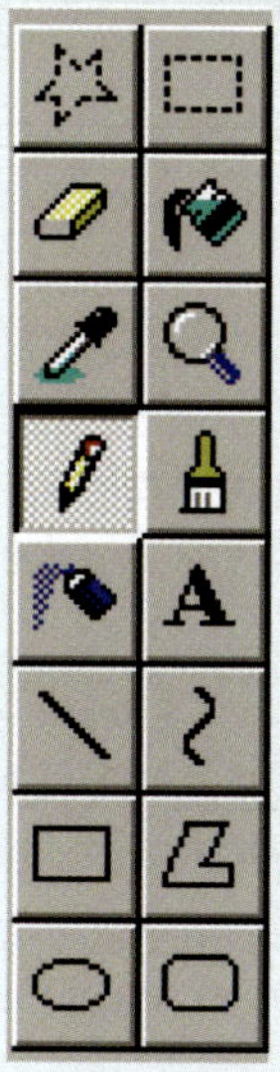

Common features:

- draw graphic
- enter text
- common tools
- alter tool attributes
- scale graphic
- rotate graphic
- crop graphic

Common tools:

- shapes – circle, ellipse, rectangle, polygon, arc, straight line
- freehand drawing – pencil, brush
- selection – arrow, rectangle, lasso, crop
- fill
- eraser
- text
- zoom

Alter tool attributes – allows the user to change the properties of the tool that they are using, for example:

- Shape – fill colour, fill pattern, fill texture

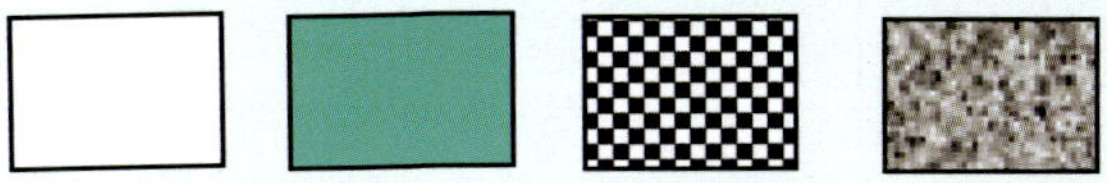

- Line – alter thickness

Scale a graphic – allows the user to change the size of the graphic. A graphic can be resized to make it smaller or bigger.

Rotate graphic – allows the user to turn the graphic in a different direction.

General question 1

a) Sally has just written an essay about her activities in the Christmas holidays. She has created this graphic to go with her essay:
Name three graphics tools which Sally has used to create the graphic. {PS 3}

b) Sally's essay takes up just over a page. What could she do to her graphic so that her essay fits on to one page? {PS 1}

a) Straight line tool, circle tool and text tool.
b) She could scale the graphic – she would resize it to make it smaller.

General question 2

Three different labels have been designed:

a) Explain what has been done to the arrow on label 1 to produce the arrow on label 2. {PS 1}

b) State two ways in which the arrow graphic on label 3 has been edited from label 1. {PS 2}

c) State two attributes that have been altered in arrow 1 to give arrow 2. {PS 2}

a) Rotated through 180°
b) Scaled (reduced in size), copied
c) Increase line thickness and fill with pattern.

Look out for

Where the line thickness has been increased, many candidates incorrectly state that the line or shape has been made bold.

What you need to know at **Credit** level ...

Scan and edit graphic – scanners can be used to input graphics (often photographs). Once a graphic has been scanned, the scanner software allows very limited editing facilities. The most common feature is the cropping feature. More detailed editing would require the use of a graphics package.

Crop graphic – allows the user to select part of the graphic.

Credit question

An image has been scanned, and part of the image is cropped. Explain what is meant by cropping a graphic. {KU 1}

Cropping removes an unwanted part of the graphic.

Look out for

Questions relating to calculating the size of a black-and-white bit-mapped graphic are often linked with this question (see 'Low-level machine', page 82).

Look out for

Make sure you understand the difference between scaling and cropping – with scaling the complete graphic remains, it is just reduced or increased in size, whereas cropping removes an unwanted part of the graphic.

Desk-top publishing

What you need to know at **General** level ...

- wizard or template
- enter text
- add clip art
- import graphic
- scale graphic.

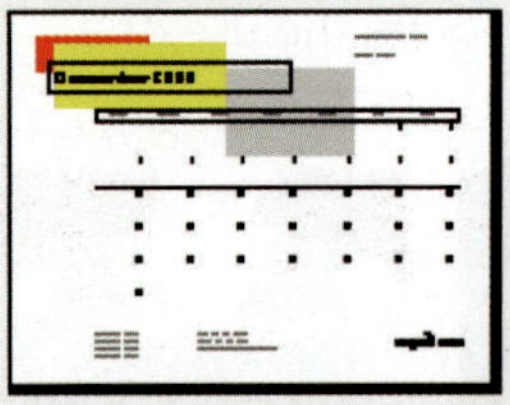

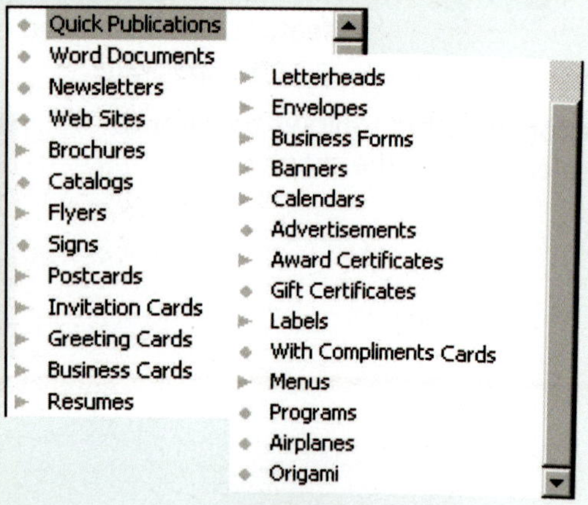

A desk-top publishing package allows the user to combine text and graphics easily and effectively to produce a variety of professional-looking documents including newsletters, flyers, posters, greetings cards and calendars.

Desk-top publishing packages include a selection of **templates** and **wizards** to provide examples of layouts and help speed up the process of document creation.

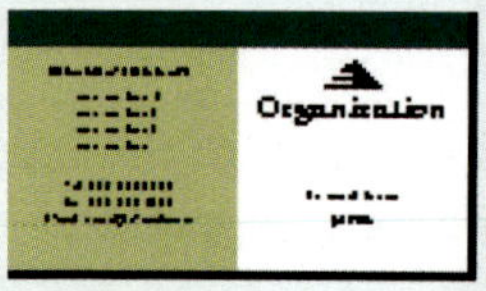

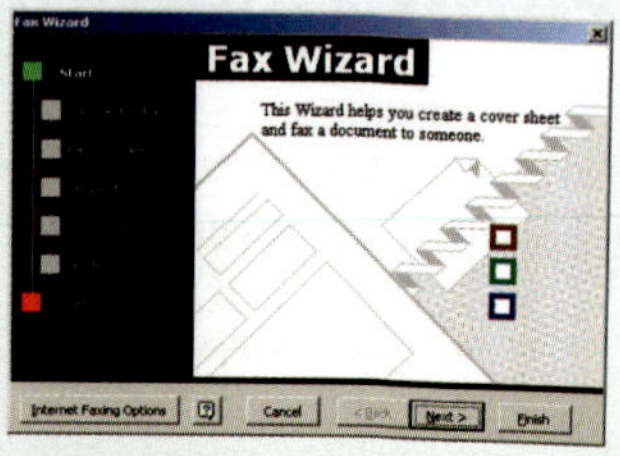

Look out for

Wizards and templates were described in GPPs.

Importing graphics

Desk-top publishing packages supply a library of clip art, but these images may not be of suitable quality. Making a document look professional often requires the use of more realistic images. To **import** a graphic means bringing in a graphic that was created using a different piece of software.

The file may have been created in another type of package or captured using a scanner or digital camera. It is important, therefore, that the user is aware of the file format of the imported image to make sure it is in a format recognised by the DTP package.

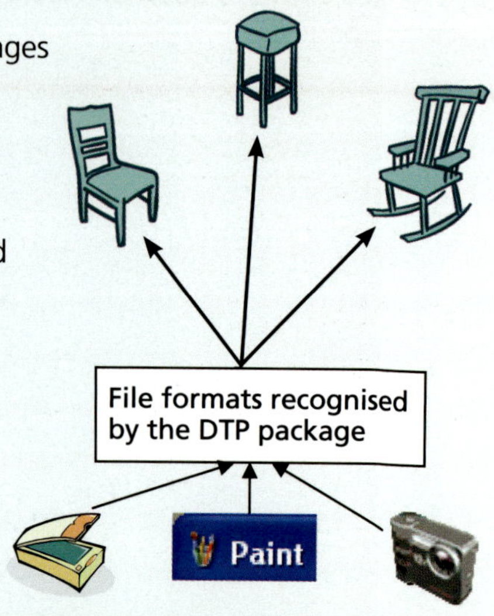

Scaling graphics

Once imported, scaling can be applied to the image to make it bigger or smaller so that it fits the selected area.

General question

a) A template could be used to speed up the creation of many publications.
   (i) What is a *template?* {KU 1}
   (ii) Suggest three types of publication where the user might use a template. {KU 3}

b) It is often necessary to scale a graphic that has been imported. Explain the terms 'import a graphic' and 'scale a graphic'. {KU 2}

a) (i) A template is a ready-made document with structure in place to hold data such as text and graphics.
   (ii) Greetings card, calendar, business card, brochure, newsletter ...

b) Import a graphic means to bring the graphic in from another piece of software. For example, the user may have created a graphic using a painting package or scanned it in. The graphic is saved and imported into the publication, where it may have to be scaled, i.e. made smaller or bigger to fit the area set aside for the picture.

Look out for

When text is being imported from a different type of package, such as a word-processing package, a **common file format** is necessary so that the file can be recognised by both types of package. Remember that common file formats for text include RTF, ASCII or TXT.

What you need to know at **Credit** level ...

- change layout
- import text
- text wrap around graphic.

Change layout

At any time during the creation of a document, the layout can be changed quickly and easily by dragging and resizing the different text and graphics boxes.

These two publications contain exactly the same data; it is just the layout that has been changed.

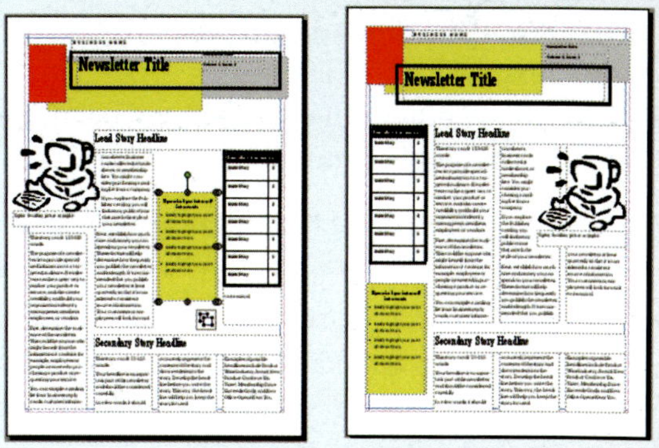

Importing text

If a text file already exists, it can be imported into the DTP document rather than the user having to enter the text again using the keyboard.

Text wrap around graphic

The two wrapping styles 'square' and 'tight' are both examples of text being wrapped around a graphic.

Wrapping text around a graphic is aesthetically pleasing to the eye and saves space.

Look out for

There are three similar terms that can be confused with each other:

- Text wrap – where text is wrapped around a graphic.
- Word wrap – instead of part of a word appearing at the end of one line and the end of the word appearing at the start of the next line, the whole word is automatically moved to the start of a new line.
- text flow – text that will not fit into one text box flows into the next text box when the two boxes are connected. Connecting text boxes is commonly used in desk-top publishing, especially when the text appears in columns.

Credit question

a) Using the document shown for ABC High School, describe where the following features have been used.
   (i) Text wrap around a graphic. {PS 1}
   (ii) Text flow. {PS 1}

b) State two methods that might have been used to produce the text in this publication. {PS 1}

a) (i) The text-wrap feature has been used in the second graphic (vegetables) but not in the first graphic (building).
(ii) The two text boxes in the top half of the page have been connected to allow text to flow automatically from the first text box to the second.

b) Method 1: Create text boxes and enter the text.
Method 2: Import the text from another file.

Presentation and multimedia

What you need to know at General level ...

Features

- wizards and templates
- linear linkage of slides
- add audio
- add video
- hyperlinks.

Look out for

Note that, although wizards and templates are features of multimedia presentation packages, they have already been described in the GPP and DTP sections and are also a feature of web-page creation.

A **multimedia presentation package** enables the user to present information on one or more slides using a variety of data types including text, graphics, sound, animation and video.

These slides are viewed in sequence (**linear linkage of slides**) unless features such as hyperlinks or action buttons are used.

Types of **template** that might be used in multimedia presentations include:

1. The **master slide layout**

This template allows the user to enter any text, graphics or action buttons that they want to appear on every slide. Font details and background colours can also be chosen on the slide master.

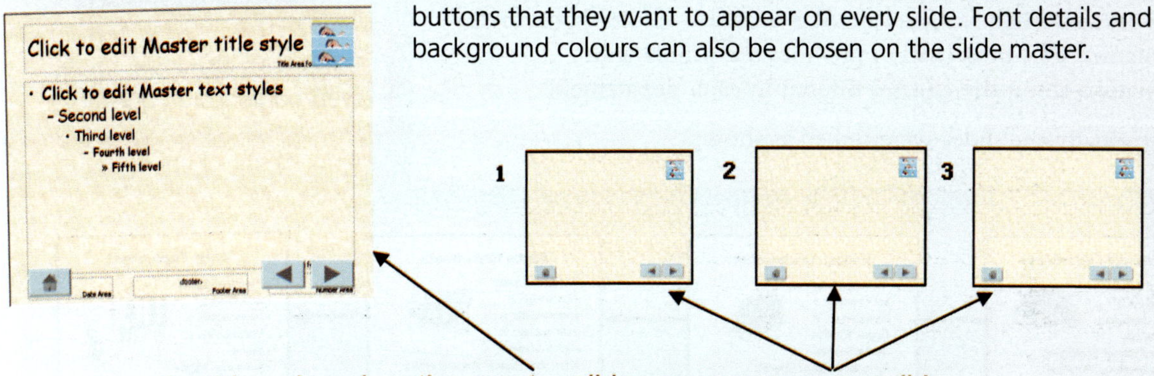

Anything placed on the **master** slide appears on **every** slide

2. **Slide layout**

A variety of different slide-layout templates are available to the user, who can choose from text-only layouts or templates with holders for graphics, media clips, charts, tables etc.

Adding sound

Sound can be added from a sound library or a pre-recorded audio CD. An audio file can be added by creating a hyperlink which will load the sound file, or the audio file can be embedded to make it part of the presentation. Sound can make a presentation more informative and interesting, or can provide appropriate sound effects to a slide.

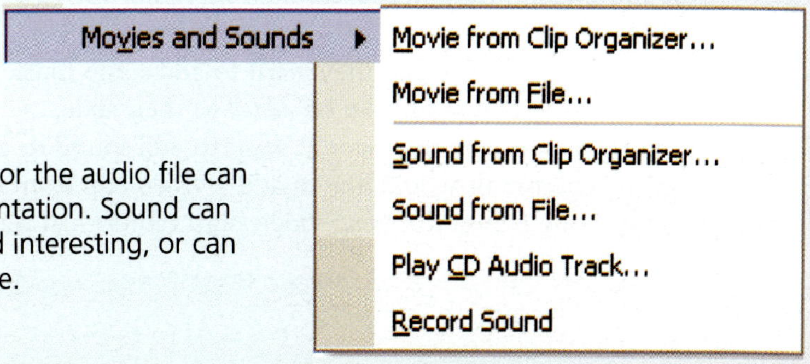

Adding video

Video can be added to make presentations more interesting or to provide information that would be difficult to put across in a still graphic.

Hyperlinks

Instead of viewing the slides in sequence, it may be desirable to view them in a different order. This can be done by creating hyperlinks which, when clicked, can take the user to another slide, an existing file, an existing web page or an e-mail address.

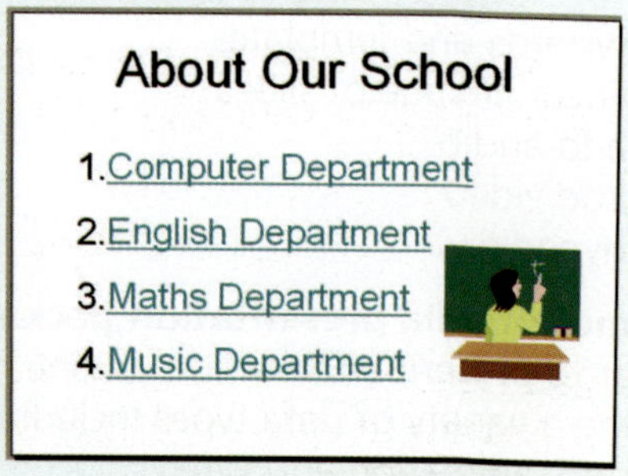

A hyperlink can be created from an area of a slide such a word, phrase or graphic. Hyperlinks are often used in a menu or index so that the user can go directly to a particular slide.

Recognising a hyperlink – if the hyperlink is a piece of text, the text colour might change and the text may be underlined. When the mouse pointer is hovered over a text hyperlink or graphic hyperlink, the arrow changes to a hand.

General question

Look out for

Hyperlinks also come up in web-page design questions.

Pupils at ABC High School can view a course-choice multimedia presentation. The presentation provides the pupils with information about the courses offered in each department.

a) Originally, the slides were linked as shown:

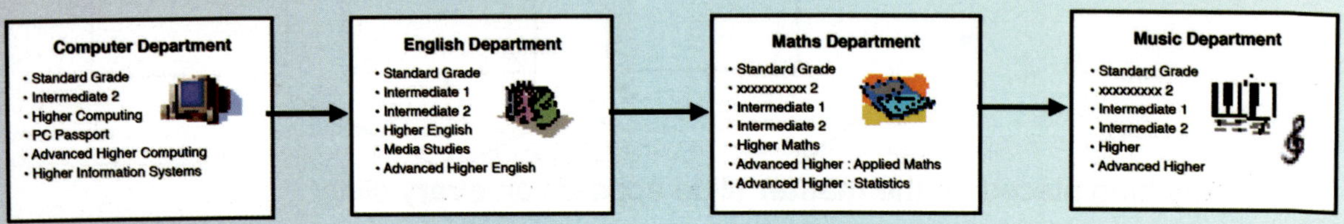

(i) State the type of linkage used. {KU 1}

(ii) To allow the user to move to the first slide, the next slide and the previous slide, it was decided to add the appropriate action buttons. Suggest one method of adding these buttons to each of the slides. {PS 1}

(iii) One of the pupils suggested that the presentation could be improved if the user was able to select only the subjects they were interested in, rather than viewing every subject. Explain how this could be done. {PS 1}

b) The music department decided they want to add some music or sound to their slide.

(i) State two ways that audio can be *added* to their slide. {KU 2}

(ii) Give one reason why they would want to add sound to their slide. {PS 1}

c) The English department would like to add a video clip from the play that the fourth-year class are studying. Give one reason for using video clips rather than photographs. {PS 1}

a) (i) *Linear linkage.*
(ii) *Add the action buttons to the master slide template. The action buttons only have to be created once on the master slide, and they will automatically appear in exactly the same place on every slide.*
(iii) *By creating a menu which contains a hyperlink for each department (see slide on previous page – About Our School).*

b) (i) *Taking it from a sound library or an audio CD.*
(ii) *To add interest or provide information not possible from any of the other types of media. For example, the music department's slide might add sound clips of the pupils' musical compositions.*

c) *A video clip of the play would allow the pupils to hear and see expression that could not be portrayed by a photograph.*

What you need to know at Credit level ...

Capture audio – sound can be captured by using a

- microphone
- digital video camera (records moving images and sound)
- mobile phone (with recording facility).

Capture image – images can be captured using a

- scanner
- digital camera / digital video camera
- webcam
- mobile phone (with camera).

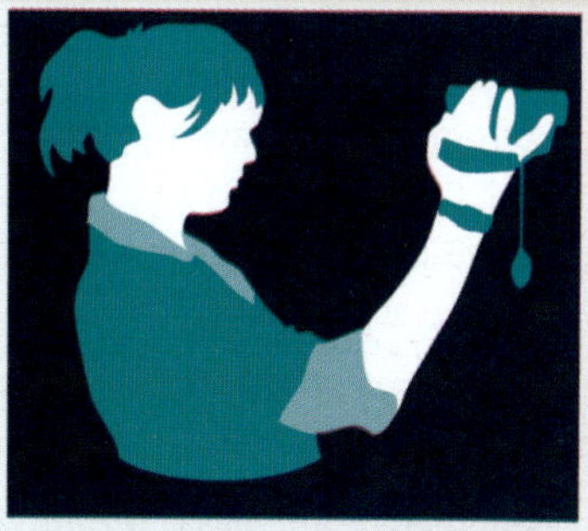

Look out for

Methods for capturing audio and images are often asked in questions relating to web-page creation. What you need to know about capturing these data types is the same for both presentation and web-page creation packages.

Look out for

All the questions below have been asked in a Credit paper, even though they are not all Credit-level questions.

Look out for

Note the difference between **adding** sound and **capturing** sound:

- **adding** sound is possible if the sound clip already exists in digital form from a source such as a library or a pre-recorded audio CD, whereas
- **capturing** sound converts naturally occurring sound, such as someone speaking, singing or playing a musical instrument into a digital format that can then be added to a presentation.

Credit question

Sixth-year pupils have been asked to put together a slide show of the school events they were involved with during the session, to be shown during the interval at prizegiving. They have video clips and pictures of their team-building day, the Christmas disco and their sixth-year dance. They also have sound recordings of the band night and talent show.

a) They decide to select a template for their slides. Give one advantage of using a template for their slide show. {KU 2}
b) What makes this a multimedia presentation? {K1}
c) They want the slide show to run automatically during the interval, displaying each slide for 30 seconds. Will the *hyperlink* feature or the *linear linkage of slides* be more appropriate for this presentation? Explain your answer. {PS 1}
d) Suggest two ways in which audio could have been captured for the presentation. {KU 2}
e) Suggest two ways in which images could have been captured for the presentation. {KU 2}
f) Give one reason for using the master slide during the creation of the slide show. {PS 1}

a) A template will speed up the creation of the slide because there is already a structure in place to hold text, graphics and other media elements.
b) The presentation is multimedia because it uses a variety of media elements such as video and graphics (from their team-building day) and sound (from the talent show).
c) Linear linkage, as the slides are to be shown one after the other in the order they were created.
d) Devices such as a mobile phone or a digital video camera (both capable of recording sound and video) or a microphone connected to a computer.
e) Digital camera or a mobile phone. Digital video cameras can also take still pictures, but the resolution is usually less than that of a digital still camera.
f) Some elements appear on every slide such as actions buttons, school name or school logo. The advantages of adding these to the master slide are: it is quicker to create slides because objects that appear on every slide only have to be added once. Also, it provides a more consistent format for the slides, as common elements appear in exactly the same place on every slide.

Web-page creation

What you need to know at General level …

Features of web-page creation

- use wizard or template
- add audio and video
- hyperlinks.

Web pages can be **created** by using:

- Web-page creation software. Examples of software that may be used in your school include Microsoft Front Page, Serif Web Plus and Macromedia Dreamweaver.
- A text editor to enter Hyper-Text Markup Language code (HTML).
- A word-processor such as Microsoft Word that allows the user to save a document as a web page.

Look out for

In a recent exam, candidates gave very poor explanations of the ways in which the selected type of multimedia could improve the website.

Look out for

No General-level questions have been included, as they are the same as the questions for multimedia – just a different scenario.

Just as **presentation** software is used to store multimedia information on **slides** to be viewed as a **slide show**, so **web-page creation** software is used to store multimedia information on **web pages** to be viewed over the **internet**.

Due to these similarities, all the Foundation and General-level features of presentation and multimedia are also features of web-page creation and include: use wizard or template; add audio, video or hyperlinks.

(For more information on these features, see the topic on presentation and multimedia.)

A selection of web-page templates

What you need to know at Credit level …

- add table
- add hotspots.

Add table

A table in a web page is similar to a table in a word-processor or an area of a spreadsheet, as they all display rows, columns and cells. The cells in a web-page table can contain data, images or hyperlinks.

Alan	Benchley	12112
Jade	Carroll	5654
Pete	Chadden	8765
Sue	Sayell	43543
Jenny	Taylor	4534
Andrew	Walker	23
Kate	Walker	94
Paul	Walker	143

English	French	Picture
apple	pomme *f*	
grapes	raisin *m*	
orange	orange *f*	

Tables can improve the appearance of a web page, as they help to organise the data into rows and columns, making the data neater and easier for the user to read.

Add hotspots

A hotspot is an area of a web page that has a hyperlink or a piece of code attached to it. Hotspots react to an event such as the mouse pointer moving over the hotspot area or a mouse click.

Hotspots are most commonly used to display hidden images or text but can be used to redirect the user to, for example, another part of the web page or to another web page.

Identifying a hotspot

Unlike a text hyperlink, which may be underlined and a different colour from the rest of the text, a hotspot is invisible. A hotspot is identified by one or more of the following:

- The screen pointer changing from an arrow to a hand in a mouse-over operation
- The contents of the hotspot being displayed (text or image)
- If the hotspot has a hyperlink attached to it, moving to the area, document or web page contained in the hyperlink.

Most application packages use hotspots to provide a textual description for toolbar icons.

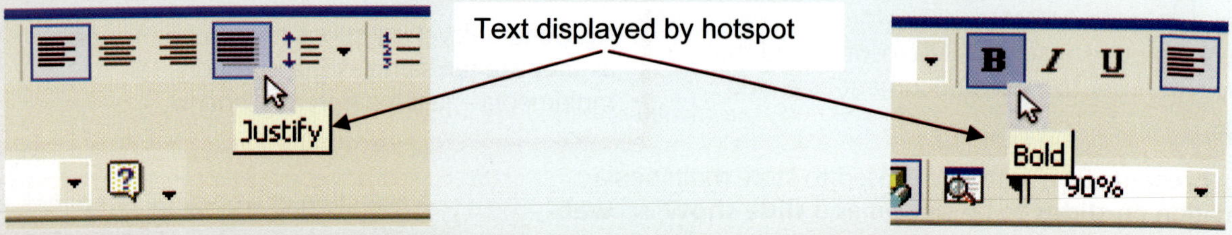

Look out for

A hotspot on a web page is a **screen** hotspot – not to be confused with a **Wi-Fi** hotspot, which is an area where wireless network signals are received.

Look out for

Websites use both hyperlinks and hotspots, so be aware of their similarities and differences.

Credit question

a) What data in the web page is held in a table? {PS 1}
b) State an advantage of using a table. {KU 1}
c) The web page on 'Backing Storage' contains several hotspots; hotspot 1 displays an image of a CD-ROM, and hotspot 2 redirects the user to another web page that has more information on USB flash drives. Where do you think these hotspots are on the page? {PS 2}
d) State one way the user can tell that the web page has hotspots. {KU 1}

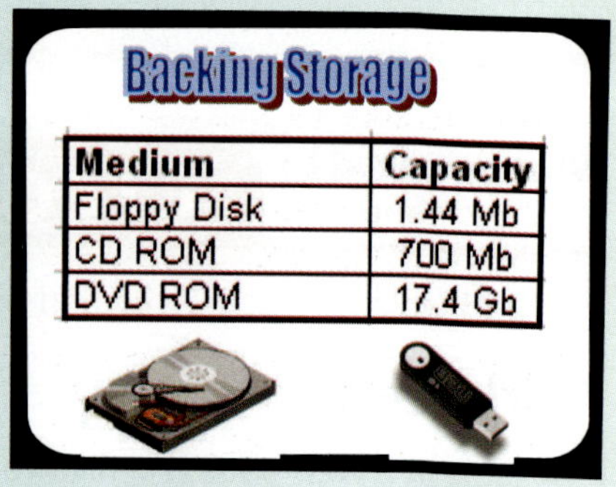

a) *The medium and capacity of floppy discs, CD-ROMs and DVD-ROMs.*
b) *A table keeps data neat and organised, thus improving the overall appearance of the web page.*
c) *Hotspot 1 – the word 'CD-ROM' in the table; hotspot 2 – the area surrounding and including the image of a USB flash drive.*
d) *When the mouse hovers over a hotspot, the mouse pointer changes to a hand.*

Expert systems

What you need to know at General level …

- purpose of expert systems
- application of expert systems.

A **human expert** is someone who is a specialist in a specific field of study.

Purpose of an expert system

An **expert system** is software which attempts to simulate a human expert. It has a user interface, an inference engine and a knowledge base to make decisions and offer advice on a particular topic.

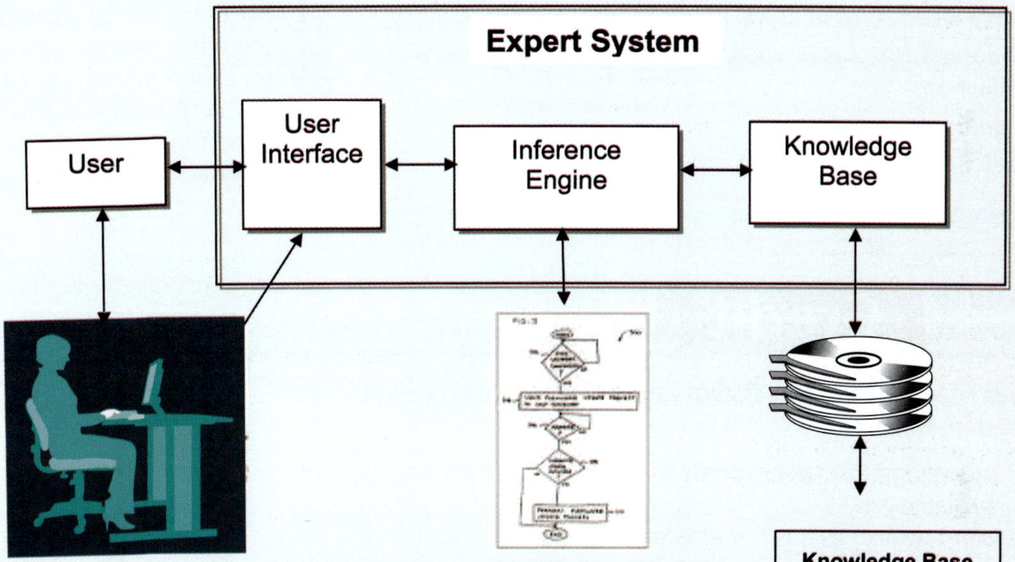

- The interface allows the user to communicate with the expert system.
- A **knowledge base** is the part of an **expert system** which contains the knowledge, often represented as **facts** and **rules** about a particular subject.
- An inference engine queries the knowledge base to reason and draw conclusions.
- **Prolog** is an example of a logic-programming high-level language which can be used to create a knowledge base.

Knowledge Base
Facts:
parent(sue,tom).
parent(bert,tom).
female(sue).
Rules:
mother(X,Y) if
parent(X,Y) and
female(X).

Application of expert systems

There are many areas where expert systems can be used, for example:

- Medicine – diagnose and treat medical ailments and diseases.
- Car mechanics – diagnose and fix car engine faults.
- Building computers – advise the technicians on suitable components to build a computer system to a particular specification.
- Geological – help to search for mineral deposits.

The local garden centre provides its customers with access to a computer which runs an expert system.

a) Explain in detail what an expert system is. {KU 2}
b) Suggest how an expert system might be used in this situation. {PS 1}
c) (i) Where else might an expert system be used? {KU 1}
(ii) What would it be used for in this situation? {KU 1}

a) *An expert system is software that extracts information from the user and data from the knowledge base to make decisions and offer advice on a particular subject area.*
b) *The expert system could be used to provide customers with advice on which plants would be suitable for their garden. The user might be asked about: soil type, sun or shade, when they want the flowers to bloom, colour etc.*
c) *(i) In a garage.*
(ii) To help the mechanics to diagnose car faults.

Look out for

For the last four years (2006–9), there has been a question on expert systems at General or Credit level – and in both papers in 2007.

What you need to know at **Credit** level ...

Advantages of using an expert system rather than a human expert: an expert system can

- hold the knowledge of many experts
- be made available 24/7
- give consistent advice, as it is not affected by personal issues
- be accessed via the internet from anywhere in the world
- be relatively cheap to operate and maintain
- preserve human experts' knowledge.

Give three advantages to the local garden centre of using an expert system to provide their customers with advice rather than employing a human expert. {PS 3}

- *The system can hold the knowledge of more than one expert.*
- *The system will be available to the customer the whole time the centre is opened, as it does not need lunch breaks or holidays.*
- *Compared with paying the wages of a human expert, the expert system is cheaper to operate and maintain.*

Look out for

In previous exams, many candidates had little or no knowledge of this topic at either General or Credit level.

Electronic communication

What you need to know at General level ...

Two methods that allow electronic communication are:

1. Electronic mail (e-mail)

Electronic mail is a method used to send a message over the internet. Internet Service Providers (ISPs) provide all the necessary e-mail services.

Advantages

- Much faster than ordinary post; arrives instantly, rather than taking days.
- More convenient for both sender and recipient than using the telephone, as the e-mail can be sent at a time suitable to the sender and can be read at a time suitable to the recipient.
- Distribution lists allow an e-mail to be sent to many recipients simultaneously.
- Mailbox can be accessed from home, work or even the other side of the world.

Disadvantages

- Junk e-mail (spam) can be extremely annoying, as time is wasted trying to differentiate junk mail from other mail and can fill up your mailbox.
- The person you are mailing needs a mailbox system.
- Must check mailbox regularly.
- Can be impersonal.

2. Text messaging – using a mobile phone. This is a quick and relatively cheap method of sending short messages. Many people not only have a mobile phone but also carry it with them most of the time.

Netiquette (network etiquette) – following a code of conduct so that people are treated with respect. Below are some netiquette rules:

- E-mails should not be more than a few lines. If it is necessary to communicate more information, an attachment should be used.
- Avoid using capital letters (SHOUTING).
- Do not say anything insulting about anyone, as once you have sent an e-mail its contents can be saved, printed or forwarded to the person.
- Large attachments should not be sent without giving the recipient prior warning and could fill up their mailbox, thus preventing them from receiving any other e-mails.

General question 1

a) State one way the following can be used for electronic communication:
   (i) Computers. {KU 1}
   (ii) Mobile phones. {KU 1}

b) Suggest a situation where a person may want to access their e-mails from somewhere other than their home or place of work. {PS 1}

c) Give two reasons why is it sensible to check your mailbox regularly. {KU 2}

a) (i) E-mail, so long as the computer has communications software and network or (preferably) internet access and the user has a subscription to an e-mail service.
(ii) Text messaging.
b) On public transport while travelling to or from work, or from another country while on holiday.
c) 1. You may have been sent an important message.
2. Your mailbox may become full, preventing you from receiving any more messages.

General question 2

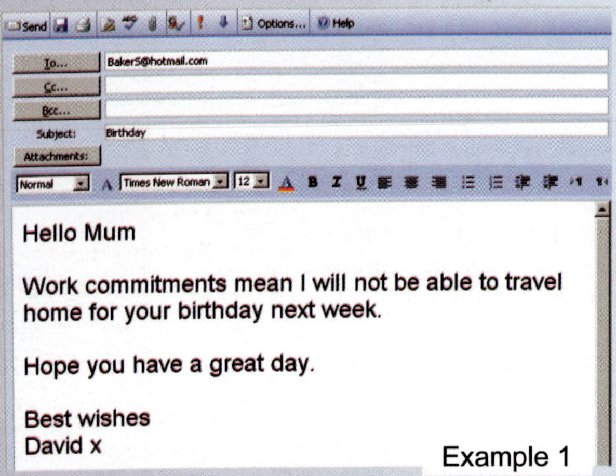

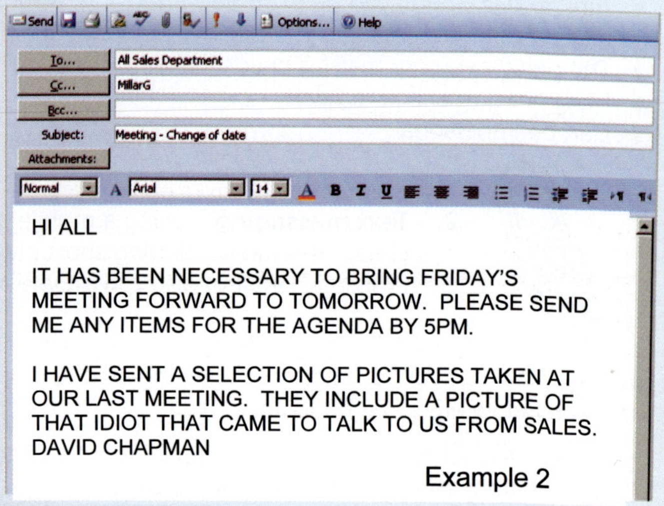

a) One of the e-mails above has broken some netiquette rules.
   (i) What is meant by netiquette? {KU 1}
   (ii) Which e-mail has broken three netiquette rules, and what are they? {PS 3}

b) From the content of Example 2, suggest two advantages of using e-mail. {PS 2}

c) From the content of Example 1, suggest two disadvantages of using e-mail rather than conventional mail. {PS 2}

a) (i) A set of rules suggesting how users should behave towards each other while using the internet.
(ii) E-mail 2. 'Shouting' (capital letters), sending large attachments ('a selection of pictures') and talking disrespectfully about others ('that idiot').

b) Sending e-mail to many recipients at the same time ('hi all'). E-mail arrives immediately (important message that needs to reach recipients as soon as possible – meeting is now tomorrow).
c) Impersonal; with personal messages, it would be much nicer to have a handwritten card or letter. The person you are sending it to must have a computer and an e-mail account.

What you need to know at **Credit** level …

File transfer – attachments

File transfer using an attachment is another method that allows electronic communication. An attachment is a file sent with an e-mail. E-mails are usually short, text-only messages. If larger text files or image files are to be sent, attachments are used to send these files over the internet alongside an e-mail message.

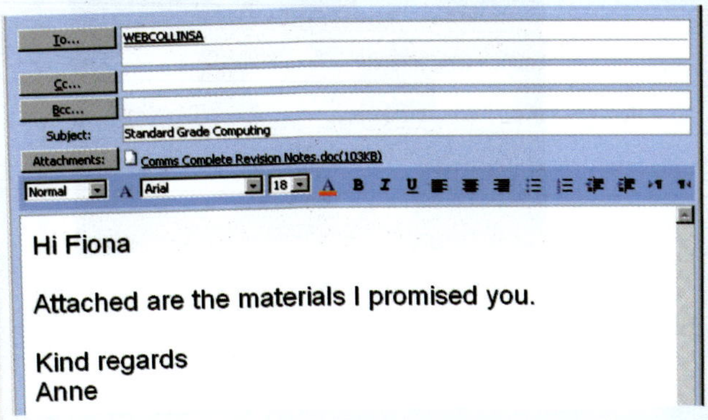

Paperclip icon alerts recipient that there is an attachment with the e-mail

Credit question

Which of the e-mails in General question 2 makes use of an attachment? {PS 1}

Example 2, where the attachment facility was used to send pictures taken at the last meeting.

Local and wide-area networks

What you need to know at **General** level ...

LANs and WANs

- description
- advantages
- transmission media
- security

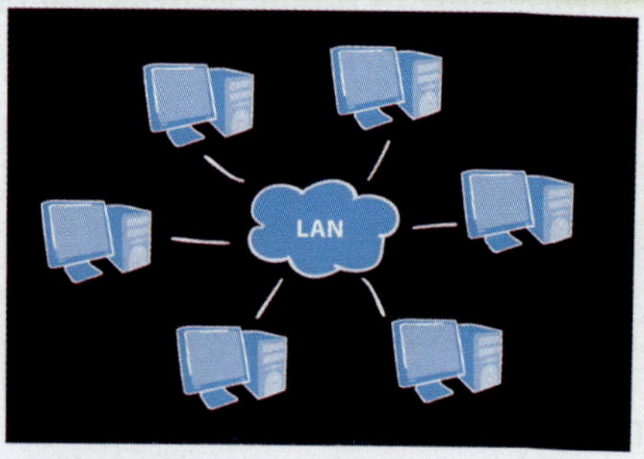

LAN – local-area network

Local-area networks are networks where a number of computers are connected to each other over a limited physical area such as a room, a building or a group of buildings in close proximity.

Advantages of a LAN

- Workstations can share expensive hardware devices such as high-quality printers.
- All users can access the same up-to-date databases and other files.
- Provides security by allowing different levels of access to different users.
- Users can access their files from any computer on the network.
- Can provide e-mail facilities.

Transmission media for LANs can be split into two types: **cable** and **wireless**.

Transmission media	Cable	Wireless
Types	Twisted-pair copper wire cables Optical fibre cables	Infra-red Bluetooth Wi-Fi
Advantages ☺	Better security Faster transmission of data (access and download) More reliable connection	Cheaper to set up/install, as cables do not have to be run Easy to expand network Increased portability No wires to trip over
Disadvantages ☹	Not cheap or easy to expand network 	Security issues (easier to hack into) Signal strength could be an issue over larger distances Signal could be blocked by a building or other object Possible health issues Slower access/download

Look out for

Disadvantages of wireless networks – candidates' responses to this question have been vague in previous exams.

WAN – wide-area networks are networks that cover a larger geographical area such as a city, a country, a continent or the world.

Advantages of a WAN

WANs have similar advantages to LANs, except that WANs do not share peripherals such as printers. An additional advantage of a WAN is that it has a much wider geographical area for accessing files (including databases) and sending e-mails. The internet is an example of a WAN.

Transmission media for WANs

- public telephone links
- microwave
- satellite links
- optical fibre cables

Security on a network

Passwords ••••••••	Encryption *hjcvza*	Physical security
• Users should frequently change their passwords and choose one that is difficult for anyone to guess • Can be used to provide different levels of access	Puts data into code before it is sent over the network and decoded at the other end (often used for sending confidential e-mails and attachments over a network)	• Locking computers and locking doors to computer room • Use a swipe card to gain entry to a computer room • Using biometric methods (fingerprints, iris or retina scans, face recognition or voiceprints)

General question

Moira is one of the managers for a large chain of Scottish supermarkets called AlwaysFresh. She regularly e-mails staff at the other branches.

a) Is the network she is using a LAN or a WAN? Explain your answer. {PS 2}

b) Some of the e-mails Moira sends are highly confidential.
   (i) What could she do before sending these messages? {KU 1}
   (ii) Suggest a physical security method that could be used to prevent unauthorised access to Moira's computer.

c) It has been decided to fit out one of the training rooms with a computer network. The computer engineer is consulted to find out if it would be better to install a wireless network or one that is connected with cables. {KU 1}
   (i) State two reasons for selecting a wireless network. (KU 2}
   (ii) State one disadvantage of a wireless network. {KU 1}

a) WAN, because Moira is able to e-mail supermarkets all over Scotland.

b) (i) Encrypt the data before sending it.

(ii) She could lock her computer or her door when she goes out of the office.

c) (i) Prevents cables having to be installed, which can be messy and expensive. Easier to expand or move to another room at a later date.

(ii) Slower access and download time.

Look out for

In previous years, when candidates have been asked specifically about **physical** security, answers given have been about any of the security methods.

What you need to know at Credit level ...

- multi-access
- network interface card (NIC)
- client-server network
- social, legal and ethical issues.

A client-server network has one or more servers whose resources can be accessed by the workstation (client). A LAN or a WAN is an example of a client-server network.

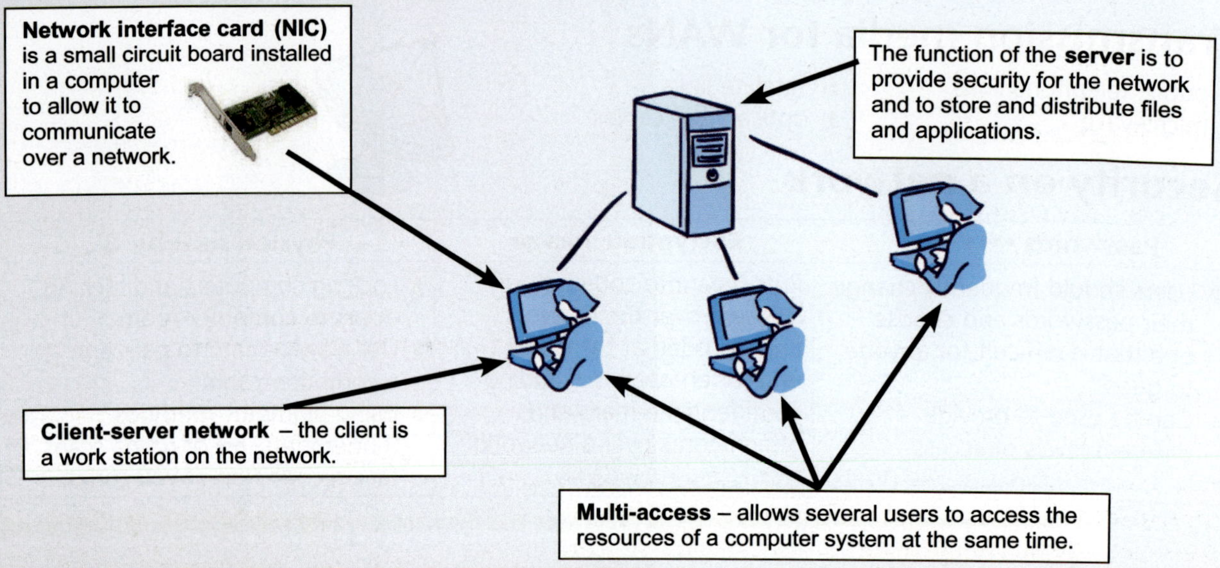

Social issues

- **Working from home** – teleworking allows people to work from home by using a wide-area network to keep them in easy contact with their workplace.

  Implications:
  - Flexible working hours
  - No travel time/costs/pollution
  - Company does not have to provide office space or facilities
  - Increased isolation / could be difficult to stay on task.
- Keeping in touch with family and friends in remote locations or abroad by using e-mail, webcams and social networking software.
- Some people cannot afford computers, broadband etc. Perhaps as more and more people communicate using a computer, those without will become more isolated.

Look out for

A common mistake is to think that a client is a user on the network. The client is the workstation – usually a desktop computer.

Legal issues

- Laws which may affect the use of computers include:
  - The Data Protection Act
  - The Computer Misuse Act
  - The Copyright, Designs and Patents Act
  - The Freedom of Information (Scotland) Act – 'A person who requests information from a Scottish public authority which holds it is entitled to be given it by the authority.' (This act does not appear in the arrangements for Computing Studies, as it only came into force in 2005; but you may be expected to know about current legislation.)

- **Ethical issues** – concerned with people's judgement as to what is right or wrong.

Look out for

The first three laws are dealt with in the section on general-purpose packages.

Credit question

A new head office is being set up for the AlwaysFresh chain of supermarkets. The managing director suggests equipping the office with stand-alone computers, as this will be cheaper than installing a client-server network.

a) (i) What is a client-server network? {KU 1}
(ii) What is a client on a network? {KU 1}
(iii) Name two additional expenses of a client-server network compared with stand-alone computers. {KU 2}

b) (i) One advantage of having a client-server network is that it can provide different levels of access. Explain how this could be an advantage for AlwaysFresh. {PS 1}
(ii) Provide the managing director with two more reasons for investing the extra money in a client-server network. {PS 2}

c) What piece of hardware will have to be installed in each computer to allow access to the client-server network? {KU 1}

d) The client-server network would provide multi-access. What would this mean for the staff? {KU 1}

e) (i) If the client-server network was part of a WAN, some staff could be given the opportunity to work from home. Give two reasons why some staff may prefer to work from home. {KU 2}
(ii) Give one advantage to AlwaysFresh of staff working from home. {KU1}
(iii) Give one disadvantage for employees and one disadvantage to AlwaysFresh of staff working from home. {KU 2}

Look out for

In past exams, many candidates did not know what a stand-alone computer was. A stand-alone computer is one that is not connected to any others by a network.

a) (i) A client-server network is a LAN or a WAN which has one or more servers whose resources can be accessed by the clients and also provides security for the network.
   (ii) A workstation.
   (iii) A server, cabling, network interface cards.

b) (i) Different members of staff could be allocated different levels of access. For example, only the managers of the company would have access to statistical information such as sales figures, staff efficiency levels etc., and only staff in the salaries department would have access to information about staff's wages.
   (ii) Staff can access their files from any workstation on the network. Files and databases can be stored centrally so that all staff can access the same up-to-date supermarket data. Allows backups to be done centrally.

c) Network interface card (NIC).

d) It would allow many staff to access the resources of the network at the same time.

e) (i) Flexible working hours – may suit staff with children. Save time and money not having to travel to work.
   (ii) Do not have to provide so many facilities – office space, heating, canteen.
   (iii) Employees – can become very isolated and it can be easy to be distracted from your work – TV, visitors, housework needing done etc. Company – difficult to get all staff together for meetings. Cost implications, as employees will have to be provided with a connection to the internet and a computer each, whereas they may have been able to share computers at work.

Look out for

Questions relating to the Computer Misuse Act are often asked as part of a network question, as it is easier to hack into and spread viruses on a network.

Look out for

Questions relating to the Data Protection Act are often asked as part of a network question, as databases with personal data are often stored on servers on a network.

Internet

What you need to know at **General** level …

Services available on the internet include WWW, e-mail, file transfer, e-commerce, online banking, online shopping, chatrooms, web logs, bulletin boards, streaming audio and video and videoconferencing.

An **internet-ready computer** includes a **modem**, a **browser** and an e-mail package.

A **modem** is a piece of hardware used to change the digital signals of the computer to the analogue signal required by the telephone line. The receiving computer requires the modem to change the analogue signals of the telephone line back into the digital signals required by the computer.

The **World-Wide Web (WWW)** is a collection of web pages held in multimedia form on computers connected to the internet. A **browser** is software that displays web pages.

HTML (Hyper-Text Markup Language) is a special language used to write web pages.

A **hyperlink** is a piece of text or a graphic that contains a link to another area on the same page, another page on the same website or another website altogether.

Search engine

A search engine is a site on the internet which helps the user search for information on a particular topic by allowing keywords to be entered. A list of possible websites is produced by the search engine.

Search engine with simple search

A simple search (also known as a basic search) is when the user enters one word (keyword) or one phrase into a search engine.

Simple search (laptop computers)

Dial-up and broadband are two ways of connecting to the internet. Some of the differences between dial-up and broadband are:

- A dial up connection means that the modem in the computer has to dial the telephone number at the start of each connected session, whereas broadband is always on.
- A dial-up connection can be paid for by the minute.
- When using the dial-up connection, the user's telephone line is out of commission, whereas with broadband the user can still receive and make telephone calls.
- Broadband has faster access to the internet.
- You can set up a LAN in your house and share a broadband connection.

Look out for

Do not confuse the purpose of a modem and a network interface card. A modem is required when linking a computer to the telephone lines. A network interface card is required to connect a computer to a network.

Look out for

Previously, there have been very poor explanations by many candidates of what a search engine is.

Look out for

A simple (basic) search using a search engine just uses one **keyword** or phrase – there is no OR, AND or NOT in the search. This is similar to a simple search using a database, where the user only searches on one field.

Online is when the user logs on to the internet.

Offline is when the user is no longer connected to the internet or to a network.

General question

The senior managers at AlwaysFresh regularly use the internet to check out their competitors' websites. They have other supermarkets' web addresses stored in their 'Favourites' so that they can access the sites quickly.

a) The websites all start with 'WWW'. What does 'WWW' stand for? {KU 1}

b) What language is used to write the web pages on a website? {KU 1}

c) Kevin, one of the managers, wants to find out more about a new product called SoSweet but does not know the web address for the SoSweet website. Explain in detail how Kevin could find the site. {PS 2}

d) The managers all complain that the internet is really slow because they are using a dial-up connection. {KU 1}

(i) State an alternative way of connecting to the internet. {KU 1}

(ii) Other than being slow, state two other disadvantages of a dial-up connection. {KU 2}

(iii) Using some of the words below, complete the following sentence.

offline *dial-up* *online* *hyperlinks*

Kevin is __________ while he is connected to the internet. He moves from page to page by clicking on__________. When he closes the browser, he is__________. {PS 3}

a) World-Wide Web

b) HTML – Hyper-Text Markup Language

c) Kevin can use a **search engine** to carry out a **simple search** using the **keyword** SoSweet

d) (i) Use a broadband connection

(ii) Can work out very expensive if the internet is used frequently. The phone line cannot be used to make or receive calls while online.

(iii) Kevin is online while he is connected to the internet. He moves from page to page by clicking on hyperlinks. When he closes the browser, he is offline.

What you need to know at **Credit** level …

An **internet service provider** is a company that has a host computer to provide the following services:

- a connection to the internet
- storing electronic mail, web pages and files for its subscribers.

Search engine with complex search

The purpose of a search engine is to help the user find information on the internet. A complex search (also known as an advanced search) allows the user to enter more than one **keyword** or phrase. These keywords or phrases are linked using AND, OR and NOT. This makes the search much more specific to the user's requirements.

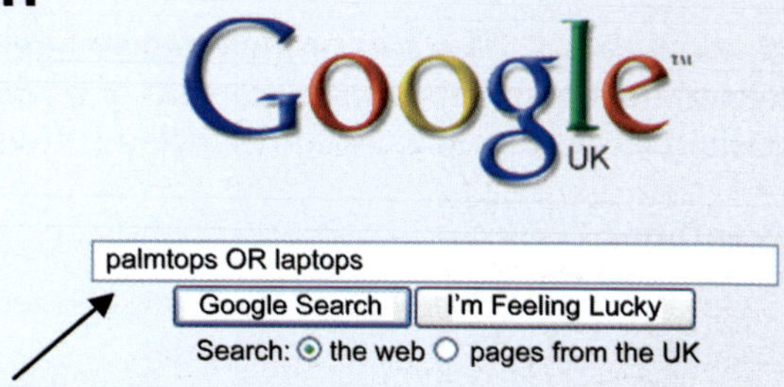

Complex search (palmtops OR laptops)

Look out for

A complex (advanced) search using a search engine is similar to a complex search using a database, where the user searches on more than one field.

Downloading software is the process of transferring data from one computer to another. Most commonly, software is downloaded from the internet to a local computer. The types of software that can be downloaded include:

- **Freeware**, which is totally free software that can be installed and used on any number of computers.
- **Shareware** means that the user can install the software for a trial period in order to evaluate it, then either the software has to be uninstalled from the computer or the user has to pay for it.
- **Commercial** software requires a licence to be purchased for each computer the software is installed on.

Mobile internet technologies – to be mobile, the technology must be capable of working without any physical connection to a power supply or the internet. Mobile technologies include:

Laptop computers

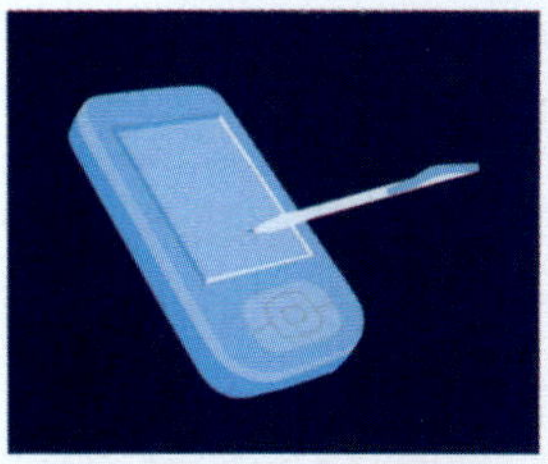

Palmtop computers

Mobile phones

A Smartphone is a mobile phone with advanced capabilities and may have some of the functions offered by a computer.

Videoconferencing

Videoconferencing is used when people cannot travel to be together but want to be able to see and talk to each other as if they were in the same room. Large companies that have offices in several locations around the country or even around the world use videoconferencing to hold meetings among the different branches of the company.

Hardware and software requirements

Each room that is to be part of the videoconference would require a computer, a network connection that linked all the computers, a video camera or a webcam, a microphone (although the camera should have recording facilities) and videoconferencing software.

Advantages

- Saves money, as there are no travelling or overnight accommodation costs.
- Saves time, as no travelling is required.
- More efficient, as employees can get straight back to work after the meeting. This would also make it possible to have more regular meetings.

Credit question

The senior managers from the different branches of AlwaysFresh occasionally travel to head office for a staff meeting, but the company has recently provided each supermarket with videoconferencing facilities.

a) Name one item of hardware and one item of software that is required for videoconferencing. {KU 2}

b) Suggest one reason why meeting using the videoconferencing facilities would benefit
   (i) the managers. (ii) the company. {KU 2}

c) Each manager has been asked to find examples of statistical analysis software that is aimed specifically at the retail trade before the next meeting.
   (i) Explain in detail how they could use the internet to find suitable software. {PS 2}
   (ii) If the software they find is freeware or shareware, they have been asked to download it onto their computer and test it out. Explain the terms *freeware* and *shareware*. {KU 2}
   (iii) Another type of software must be bought before it can be installed, and a licence is required for each computer it is installed on. What is the name of this type of software? {KU 1}

Look out for

In this topic in previous exams, candidates have seemed less sure of questions on internet service providers, and too many simply did not know about freeware and shareware.

d) Although the managers have been asked to download the software, users who do not have an internet connection can have the software distributed by post. Suggest one benefit to
   (i) the managers
   (ii) the software company
   of being able to download the software. {PS 2}

e) Why might software companies prefer to market their software as freeware rather than commercial? {PS 1}

f) Very occasionally, the managers will still have to meet face to face. Some travel by train and find it useful to use a mobile internet technology device so that they can work during the journey.
   (i) Name three such devices. {KU 3}
   (ii) Define what makes a technology mobile. {KU 1}
   (iii) State one service that an Internet Service Provider could supply for this technology. {KU 1}

a) *Hardware – video camera/webcam/microphone*
   Software – videoconferencing software such as Microsoft's NetMeeting

b) (i) *Do not have to leave early in the morning or stay overnight if they have a long way to travel*
   (ii) *More efficient, as managers will be able to return to work immediately the meeting is finished*

c) (i) *They could carry out a complex search using a search engine. Examples of the complex search include:*
   'statistical analysis software' AND 'retail trade'
   'statistical analysis software' + 'retail trade'
   (ii) *Freeware – can be installed free of charge on as many computers as the user wants*
   Shareware – can be installed for a trial period in order to evaluate it, then it must be either paid for or uninstalled
   (iii) *Commercial*

d) (i) *They can install the software immediately, whereas by post they would have to wait days.*
   (ii) *Saves them time and money. It would take time to burn software onto CD and then take it to the post office. It would cost money to buy the CDs and pay for postage.*

e) *There might be more chance of someone purchasing the software if they had the opportunity to evaluate it first.*

f) (i) *Mobile phones, smartphones, laptops and palmtops*
   (ii) *A technology is mobile if it can operate without any physical connection to mains electricity or the internet.*
   (iii) *E-mail facilities.*

Chapter 3 Industrial applications/automated systems

What you need to know at **General** level …

What is an automated system?

An automated system is a system where you provide the **input**, and the machine carries out the **process** and provides you with an **output**.

The need for automated systems

Speed	They can carry out processes much faster than humans
Hazardous environments	They can be used in places that it would be harmful or dangerous for people to work
Repetitive tasks	Humans get bored of doing the same task over and over again, and this can lead to mistakes
Efficiency	Systems can work all day without a break
Accuracy	They can do finely detailed work without getting tired and making a mistake; and, when producing items, these are all exactly the same

A **sensor** is a device which detects physical data from its surroundings.

Type of sensor	Type of task	
light	controlling street lights	
heat	controlling a central-heating system	
movement	controlling traffic lights	
bump	stopping a mobile robot if it bumps into an object	
strain	preventing a lift from being overloaded	
sound	controlling a mobile robot by clapping hands	

Feedback

- Feedback is the signal which a sensor sends back to the computer.
- The computer makes a decision based on the feedback.

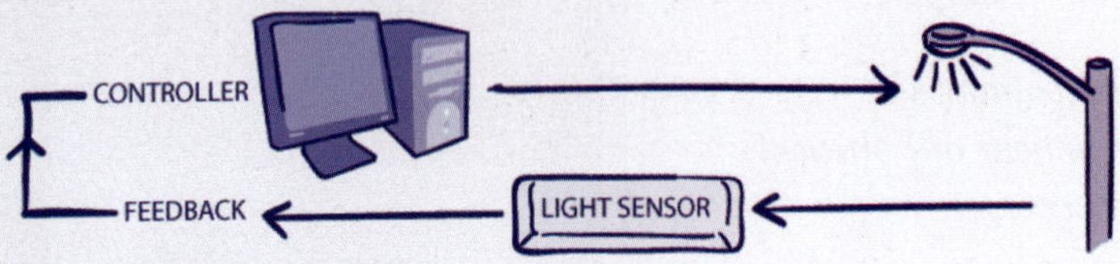

Without sensors, the street lights would switch on and off at the same time each day, irrespective of how light or dark it was.

Analogue input and output

Most sensors detect **analogue** data, but computers can only process **digital** data.

Analogue

What does 'analogue' and 'digital' mean?

An analogue signal is a signal which changes continuously, such as temperature, pressure and light, whereas a digital signal is a signal that changes in steps. An example of digital data is the display on a digital watch, where the numbers for minutes and hours jump in units of one, whereas the hands on an analogue watch are continually moving.

Digital

Interface – devices are connected to the computer by an interface. The job of the interface is to make sure that the correct signals are sent between the computer and the device, including changing the **analogue** signal of the device/sensor to the **digital** signal required by the computer.

Look out for

Do not confuse with a human–computer interface (HCI). An HCI is the interface between the **user** and the computer. A (hardware) interface is the interface between a **device** and the computer.

Look out for

Many candidates could only state one way that a robot could be taught.

Robots

Anatomy – some robots have parts that resemble human limbs. The robot shown has a waist, shoulder, elbow and wrist.

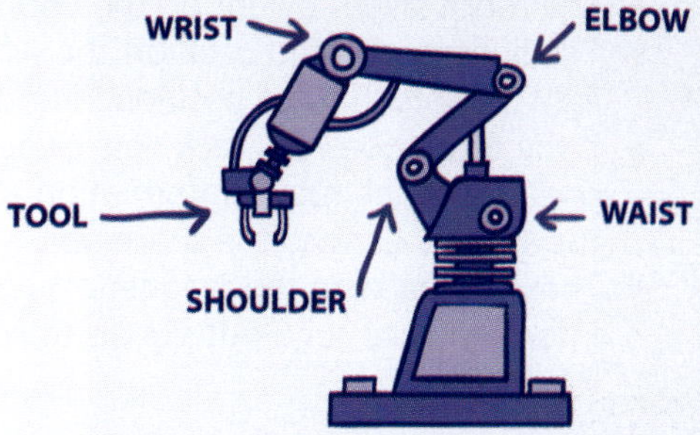

Motors power each moveable part of the robot's arm and may be either inside the robot or connected to it.

The **tool** at the end of the arm is a device to carry out a specific type of task. The tool shown on this robot is known as a gripper. Other tools include screwdrivers, spray guns, welding guns, suction pads and magnets.

Teaching robots – two methods can be used to 'teach' robots:

- **Programmable robots** are controlled by a computer program which has been coded by a programmer.
- **Programming by example** (also known as lead-through programming): an operator holds the end of the robot's arm and carries out the task (paint-spraying, welding, handling toxic materials etc.). Sensors in the robot's arm inform the computer of the sequence of movements, and this information is saved onto a backing storage device.

Stationary robots are robot arms that stay in one place all the time. They are often used on assembly lines where the products being assembled might move along a conveyor belt until they reach the required robot. **Mobile robots** move around using wheels or tracks and are usually powered by electric motors.

CAD (computer-aided design) uses a computer to design objects/layouts on a screen.

CAM (computer-aided manufacture) uses a computer to control the production of goods.

CAD	CAM	CAD/CAM
Car/road design	Making car parts	Postage stamps
Kitchen/building layout	Cutting cloth for clothes	Flags

Look out for

It is alarming how few candidates in previous exams knew what CAD stood for!

Guiding mobile robots

Two systems used to guide mobile robots are:

1. Magnetic guidance

- A cable buried in the floor gives off a magnetic field.
- Sensors suspended underneath the robot detect the magnetic field and feed the data back to the processor controlling the robot.
- The processor then uses this information to send out signals to control the direction of the robot's wheels.

2. Light guidance

- The robot shines a light on the floor.
- The light is reflected back off the white line and is picked up by light sensors that are positioned underneath the robot.
- If the robot goes off track, less or no light will be reflected from one side of the robot. Information about reflected light is fed from the sensors back to the processor.
- Then, just as with the magnetic guides, the processor uses this information to send out signals to control the movement of the robot.

Safety precautions are necessary when mobile robots are in use. Precautions include:

- fitting sensors to enable robots to detect objects in their path
- covering any moving parts
- moving slowly
- making some sort of warning sound.

Simulation is the use of a computer program to replicate a real-life situation. Two major areas where computer simulations are used are for training purposes, such as pilots and surgeons, and testing the design of new products such as cars.

Look out for

It is important to appreciate that a simulation offers interaction in a way which is beyond simply seeing what the design LOOKS like.

Virtual reality simulates a three-dimensional world digitally using software and a computer system.

Specialised devices:

Input device – a data glove.

Output device – Headset with built-in earphones and goggles.

Even without specialised input and output devices, a virtual-reality effect can be produced with software, such as some computer games, tours round shops etc.

Real-time processing is where a system responds immediately to input. This type of processing is necessary for automated systems which have feedback, simulations and virtual reality.

! Look out for

A question relating to real-time processing comes up every year.

Implications of automated systems in the workplace

Social implications include:

- When automated systems are introduced into a workplace, many people's jobs are taken over by robots. These people either become unemployed or are retrained to do different jobs.
- Staff can be retrained to operate, program and maintain the new systems.
- Could lead to increased leisure time for staff.

Economic implications

The **initial** cost of designing a new factory, buying equipment and retraining staff can be very expensive but is offset by cheaper **running** costs. Automated systems can work 24/7, don't get paid and do not require costly resources such as heating, lighting and canteen facilities, although there are equipment maintenance and replacement costs.

General question

A building merchant uses automated forklift trucks to move timber, tiles and bricks around the warehouse.

a) Give two advantages of using automated vehicles. {KU 2}

b) If a forklift truck attempts to lift more than the maximum weight, it is immediately stopped. What type of processing is being used? {PS 1}

c) There are two methods of guiding the automated forklift trucks around the warehouse. State the two methods and give one disadvantage of each. {KU 4}

d) Sensors are fitted to the vehicles so that they stop if their path is blocked in some way. What type of sensors may have been fitted? {PS 1}

e) State two safety features that could be used with the vehicles. {KU 2}

f) State two ways in which automation may change the jobs of the workers. {KU 2}

a) Save money on wages, can work 24/7 and make fewer mistakes

b) Real-time processing

c) Light guidance system – white lines can become dirty or partially covered
Magnetic guidance system – expensive, as wires have to be buried under the floor

d) Pressure sensors or motion sensors

e) Flashing light, moving very slowly or making a warning sound

f) Retrained to carry out different jobs; increased leisure time.

What you need to know at **Credit** level ...

Adaptability

Automated systems are very adaptable because they can be reprogrammed and, in the case of robot arms, fitted with different tools to enable them to carry out different tasks.

Control language

The programs written to control the robots are often written in a **control language** that the programmer can use to tell a robot which way to turn, how high to lift the gripper or how far to travel, or even to control the speed of the motor.

In a **stationary robot**, the robots are usually attached to a computer, and the control programs are stored on backing storage devices such as hard discs.

Mobile robots, on the other hand, usually have their control programs stored on a ROM chip.

Look out for

A control language is an example of a high-level language. One of the common features of a high-level language is that it is designed to carry out a specific kind of task. In this case, the language is designed with appropriate commands to control a robot, such as 'forward 50', 'right 90' and 'grasp'.

ROM software

Mobile robots on the factory floor, in outer space or down on the ocean bed cannot be physically linked to a computer, so their control programs are stored on read-only memory (ROM) chips and embedded into the robot. An **embedded system** is a piece of equipment that contains a small computer or processor chip.

Advantages of ROM compared with disc

- not easily corrupted
- software cannot be deleted accidentally
- program loads much faster.

Disadvantages

- more expensive
- to change the control program, the ROM chip will have to be replaced.

Intelligent robots should be able to learn from mistakes or adapt to new situations. They are fitted with powerful processors, large built-in memory and a variety of sensors in order to simulate intelligence.

Analogue-to-digital AND digital-to-analogue converters

Sensors detect analogue signals such as light, heat, sound and motion. In order for the computer to store these signals in digital form, an **analogue-to-digital** converter is required. When the computer outputs the data, a **digital-to-analogue** converter is required to change the digital signals of the computer to the analogue signals required by the output device.

Look out for

Too many candidates in previous exams said incorrectly that an advantage of ROM is that it is not deleted when the power is switched off. In this situation, you should compare ROM with other backing storage devices, not RAM. Other backing storage devices do not lose their data when the power is switched off.

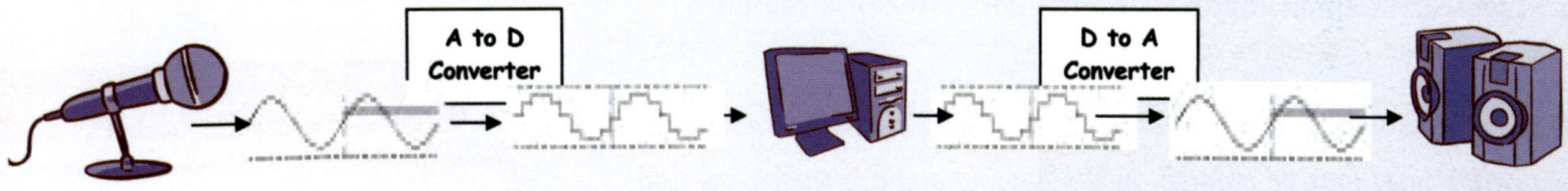

Automating a factory

Before automating a factory, a systems analysis should be carried out.

Need for systems analysis

A systems analyst is employed to examine the existing system to decide if it could be improved by automation.

Design of an automated factory

Factories that are designed mainly for automated systems can look different from factories designed mainly for humans. Changes include:

- Less heating and lighting (including fewer windows)
- Fewer facilities such as toilets, canteen facilities and water fountains
- Shelves can be placed higher than a human can reach
- A magnetic guidance system installed with wires buried beneath the floor; or, if a light guidance system is used, white lines will be painted on the floor.

Credit question

a) The building merchant's warehouse has been designed for automated forklift trucks rather than humans. Describe two ways in which a factory designed for automation would differ from one designed for humans. {KU 2}

b) The automated vehicles are fitted with bump sensors which cause the vehicle to stop if pressure is detected. Is this an example of an intelligent robot? {PS 1}

c) The vehicles are controlled using an embedded system. What is meant by an embedded system? {KU 1}

d) The control program used in the embedded system is stored on a ROM chip.
   (i) What is meant by a control program? {KU 1}
   (ii) Give two advantages of storing software in ROM. {KU 2}

e) The warehouse is not heated, and the vehicles cannot operate below a certain temperature, so they are fitted with heat sensors. Is an analogue-to-digital converter or a digital-to-analogue converter required? {PS 1}

a) White lines may be painted on the floor to guide the vehicles, and shelves might be placed much higher than can be reached by humans.

b) No, intelligent robots are able to learn from their mistakes and not just respond to inputs. In this case, the input is pressure detected by the sensor.

c) An embedded system is a piece of equipment that contains a small computer or processor chip.

d) (i) A control program is a special language designed to control the movements of an automated device.
(ii) The software cannot be deleted accidentally, cannot be corrupted by viruses and loads up very quickly.

e) An analogue-to-digital converter is required because temperature is analogue.

Look out for

In previous exams, when candidates were asked how the design of the two types of factory differed, they described how robots could be used in a factory rather than how a factory designed for humans would be different from a factory designed for robots.

Look out for

In previous exams, candidates gave poor explanations of what an embedded system is and what storage medium would be used for this type of system.

What you need to know at **General** level ...

Commercial data-processing

Commercial data processing (CDP) is how large companies and other organisations, such as supermarkets, police and utility companies, use computers in their businesses.

CDP requires **mainframe computers** that can process **large quantities** of data **very quickly** and give the user **fast access** to the data. It is essential that these systems can deal with **repetitive tasks**.

Users wanting to communicate with the mainframe do so using **terminals**. Terminals that only consist of a keyboard and a screen are known as **dumb** terminals, and if they are linked using a wide-area network they are known as **remote** terminals.

Look out for

In previous exams, many candidates did not know what a terminal was or why the supermarket needed a mainframe computer.

Look out for

The workstations (clients) on a client-server network are similar to the terminals connected to a mainframe, except that workstations tend to have their own processing power, RAM and backing storage whereas terminals often consist only of a screen and keyboard.

Advantages: compared with a manual system, a computerised commercial data-processing system is faster, more efficient and more accurate at inputting, processing, storing and outputting vast volumes of data.

A computerised system allows efficient storage of customer details, taking up much less space and with easy methods of updating data. It is also easier to maintain contact with customers using mailshots.

Data and information

Data is raw, unprocessed facts and figures which are accepted and processed by a computer system. Information is set in context and has meaning, whereas data does not mean anything on its own.

For example, it is unclear what the piece of data 180409 means until it is turned into information: Tel. No. 180409, or 18 April 2009, or Sort Code 18-04-09.

Stages of the data-processing cycle

1. Data collection and preparation

The first stages of the data-processing cycle are to collect data and prepare it in such a way that the computer can understand it.

2. Data input

Methods of inputting data include:

Mark sense cards – marks such as lines or crosses are made on mark sense cards, which are then read by a mark sense reader. Uses of these cards include multiple-choice answers and selection of lottery numbers.

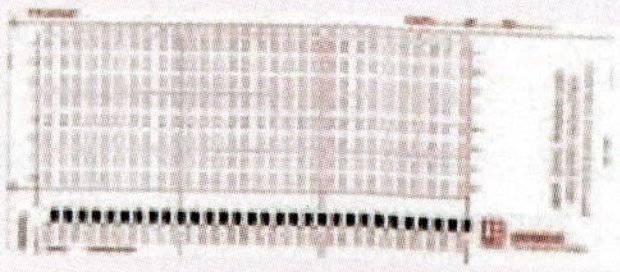

Magnetic stripe – the magnetic stripe on the card holds a very limited amount of information and can be used on credit cards, school dinner cards, train tickets etc.

Barcodes – information included on barcodes includes country of origin, manufacturer's code, product name, quantity and **check digit**.

Data from the barcode is used to link to additional information stored on the shop's database. The database information is used for stock control and setting a price for the item.

Magnetic ink character recognition – magnetic ink is used to print characters which can be read by a magnetic ink character reader. Magnetic ink characters can be found at the foot of a bank cheque.

Advantages:

- it is both human and machine-readable
- magnetic ink characters are difficult to forge
- processing is more accurate
- it is quicker to input data using the reader than for an operator to type the data in.

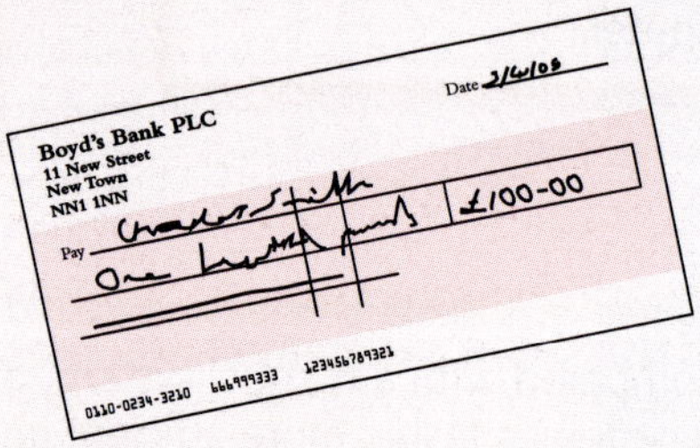

Making sure data is correct

Different types of checks can be made to help ensure that the source (original) data has been entered into the computer correctly.

Three methods include **check digits**, **range checks** and **length checks**.

Look out for

A common mistake is thinking that the price is part of the barcode. Different shops charge different prices for the same item, which is why the price cannot be included on the barcode.

Look out for

These types of check are now commonly appearing in the exam as part of a database question, where you have to identify a field that a validation check could be applied to.

Check digits – a check digit is the last digit of a number such as a barcode or an ISBN number. It is produced by performing an algorithm on the rest of the number.

When a barcode is scanned, the check digit lets the scanner determine if it scanned the number correctly or not. If the check digit it calculates is different from the one it reads, the scanner alerts the operator that something went wrong and the item will have to be rescanned.

An example of an algorithm used to create a check digit is as follows: Code **60040265937**

- Add the numbers in the odd positions together: 6 + 0 + 0 + 6 + 9 + 7 = **28**
- Multiply the total by 3: 28 × 3 = **84**
- Add the numbers in the even positions together: 0 + 4 + 2 + 5 + 3 = **14**
- Add the two totals together: 84 + 14 = **98**
- Add the smallest number that will make the total a multiple of ten: 98 + **2** =100
- So, the check digit is 2, and the code (including the check digit) is 60040265937**2**

Look out for

Many candidates in previous exams did not know how a check digit was calculated. You would **not** be expected to explain the algorithm, but you should know that the check digit is produced from a calculation using the other numbers in the code.

Length check – making sure that data such as names, catalogue numbers etc. contains no more than a specific number of characters.

Range check – a range check can be made on numeric fields, such as ages, times and dates, to ensure that the data entered is within given limits. Unacceptable data would be:

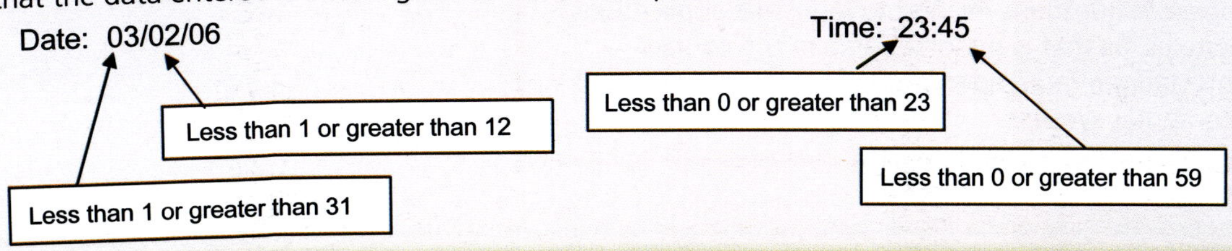

3. Data processing and storage

In large commercial systems such as airlines, mail-order companies, banks and utility companies, data is constantly being **updated**, with the results being fed back to the user in a two-way conversation. This is an example of **interactive processing**.

A backup copy is an exact copy of the original in case the original data is lost or damaged. Magnetic tape is a very common backing storage medium for storing backups, as it can store vast quantities of data very cheaply.

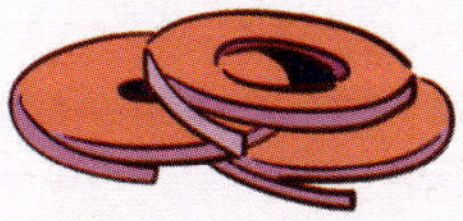

Look out for

Many candidates were unable to identify a range or validation check in past exams.

Look out for

In previous exams, when asked what type of processing was going on, many candidates failed to identify interactive processing. For this course, you only have to know about interactive and real-time (see Automated systems) processing.

Look out for

It is a common error to mix up the terms **backup** and **backing storage**. Remember that backing storage is used to permanently store data when the computer is switched off.

4. Output

Methods of output include:

- paper – printing data such as utility bills or bank statements
- screen – the same data can be displayed on a monitor, and customers can view their bills using the internet
- file – data can be saved as a file onto backing storage.

Social implications – job types and careers

- **Systems analyst**:
  - examines the current system to see if it can be improved by computerisation
  - gathers information to help with the decision-making
  - specifies the hardware and software requirements for the new system.
- **Programmer** – writes the software for the new computerised system
- **Engineer** – installs and maintains the computers
- **Network manager** – in charge of the running of the network, including installing software, making regular backups and setting users' level of access to the network.

Look out for

In previous exams, many candidates did not know the tasks performed by a systems analyst. As well as this topic, job types and careers often appear in questions relating to industrial applications or automated systems, as that is the other area in the course where computing staff are required to design, create, operate and maintain large computer systems.

Technical implications

E-commerce is a way of conducting business using a network, most commonly the internet. Two examples of e-commerce are online shopping and online banking.

- **Online shopping** – many people are choosing to shop online rather than shopping in the high street. Almost anything can be bought online, but some of the more common items include food, clothes, books, CDs, DVDs, insurance, tickets and electrical goods.

  Customers benefit because they do not have to travel or find a parking space, and they can shop in the comfort of their own home by day or night. Also, many products are cheaper online.

  Shopkeepers benefit – no expensive rates and council tax; premises can be in less central, cheaper locations; no need for sales staff or expensive catalogues.

- **Online banking** – customers can carry out many of their banking transactions using online banking facilities.
- **Electronic funds transfer** (EFT) – when shopping, customers can purchase goods by using a debit card to transfer funds electronically. The system automatically takes money from the customer's bank account and places it in the shop's bank account. Tills that are capable of this kind of transaction are called **point of sale** (POS) terminals.

The steps involved in the process of electronic funds transfer are:

- The card details are entered. The numbers are either scanned or input.
- The bank is contacted.
- The payment is authorised.
- The money is transferred.

Economic implications

Hardware, software and staff training contribute to high **initial costs** of computerising a large company. The **running costs** of a computerised system can also be significant and include electricity, paper, ink, maintenance, updating software and ongoing staff training.

Physical and software security

Due to the vast quantities of data that are input, stored and processed, it is vital that companies take responsibility for keeping the data secure. The security methods (passwords, encryption, locking computers and doors, swipe cards and biometrics) mentioned in the section on Networks are the same as the methods used for commercial data-processing.

Sale of customer lists

Some companies build up large databases of customers' names and addresses that they can sell on to other companies. These companies try to identify customers from these lists who they think might buy their goods, and send out advertising literature (junk mail).

Junk mail is bad for the environment because of the amount of paper that is generated, especially when most of it ends up being thrown away, sometimes without even being opened.

Look out for

The process of EFT was badly answered by candidates in previous exams.

Look out for

In previous exams, many candidates did not know any economic implications to the company if they went ahead with the systems analyst's recommendations.

Look out for

Questions relating to the Computer Misuse Act can be linked to this topic, as they are relevant to the security of online banking. It is an offence to gain unauthorised access to a computer system, and therefore anyone trying to access a bank account unlawfully could be prosecuted.

General question

Every day, vast amounts of data are input, processed and output at AlwaysFresh shops.

a) What type of computer would be used by the supermarket? {KU 1}

b) Vast amounts of data are input daily. Explain the difference between data and information. {KU 2}

c) (i) AlwaysFresh uses a variety of methods for inputting data. Match each input method to an appropriate task. {PS 4}

Method of input	**Task**
1. Barcodes	Used to play the national lottery
2. Mark sense cards	Processing customers' cheques
3. Magnetic stripe cards	Items are scanned at the checkout
4. MICR	Used by the staff in the canteen

(ii) Name two items of information contained in a barcode. {KU 2}

(iii) What does MICR stand for? Give two advantages of using MICR. {KU 3}

d) It is vital that there are as few errors as possible in the data input by the supermarket.

Suggest a type of check that can be done on each of the following: {PS 3}

(i)

42000 06200

(ii)

Menu
(Select 1–3)
1. Stock & Ordering
2. Salaries
3. Statistics

(iii) Mobile phone numbers:

07745932098
07854398230
07534129875

e) When the operators scan the barcode on each item, the price is displayed at the till.

(i) Is the price part of the barcode? Explain your answer. {KU 2}

(ii) What type of processing is this? {PS 1}

f) The computer department at head office employs a programmer, an engineer and a network manager. Describe one task carried out by each of these people. {KU 3}

g) Head office decides to add a new subsystem to deal with customer services. Describe one task that a systems analyst would carry out in this situation. {KU 1}

a) A mainframe computer.
b) Data does not mean anything on its own, whereas information is set in context and has meaning.
c) (i)

Method of input	Task
1. Barcodes	**2.** Used to play the national lottery
2. Mark sense cards	**4.** Processing customers' cheques
3. Magnetic stripe cards	**1.** Items are scanned at the checkout
4. MICR	**3.** Used by the staff in the canteen

(ii) Country of origin, product name, quantity and check digit.
(iii) Magnetic Ink Character Recognition. Magnetic ink characters are difficult to forge, and processing is more accurate.

d) (i) Bar code – check digit. (ii) Menu – range check (1 to 3).
(iii) Mobile phone numbers – length check (11 digits).

e) (i) No. The price is not part of the barcode, because different shops sell the same items at different prices.

f) Programmer – writes and maintains the software used by the supermarkets.
Engineer – maintains the hardware.
Network manager – sets levels of access for staff.

g) Examines the current system that deals with customer services to see where it can be improved by computerisation.

What you need to know at **Credit** level ...

Management information

Computers make it much easier to collect large quantities of data about a company so that it can be processed, collated and presented in such a way that managers can make appropriate decisions about the running of the company.

Types of useful information may include:

- budgets, including profit and loss
- staff productivity
- popularity of goods.

Look out for

Questions relating to management information proved difficult for candidates in previous years, as many of them did not know what management information meant.

Smart cards – also known as a chip and PIN card; has its own processor.

The advantages of a smart card compared with a magnetic stripe are:

- the microprocessor cannot be easily forged
- the data on the microprocessor can be updated
- it is more secure than carrying cash
- the microprocessor can hold more information.

Validation and verification

It is essential that data being input to the computer is as error-free as possible. Two methods used are:

- **Validation** ensures that the data provided is sensible. For example, a date could be checked to make sure that the day is a number between 1 and 31.
- **Verification** ensures that the data has been entered correctly, i.e. that the data entered is exactly the same as the source data. One method is double data entry – one operator enters the data, then the same data is entered again by another operator; and, if there are any discrepancies between the two sets of data, an error is reported.

Multi-user databases

A multi-user database is a database that can be accessed by many users at the same time, thus allowing users access to the same up-to-date data. A multi-user database is stored centrally on, for example, a mainframe computer or a file server on a client-server network.

Look out for

Many candidates in previous exams incorrectly called a multi-user database a 'multiple-user database'.

Sequential and random access

Sequential access means that data can only be read in the order it was written. **Direct** access means that data can be accessed in any order.

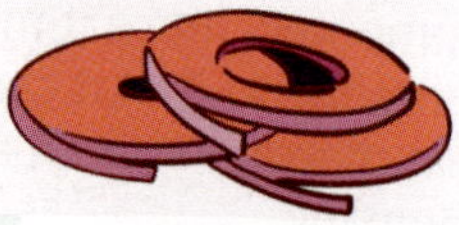
Magnetic tape

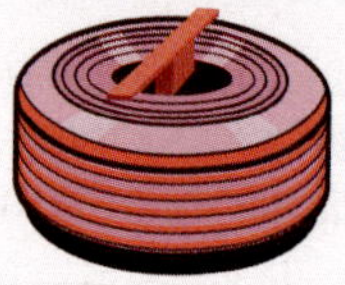
Hard disk pack

Commercial companies deal with vast amounts of data. The backing storage mediums most suited to storing large volumes of data on mainframe computers are magnetic tape and hard discs.

Magnetic tapes are cheaper but access to data is much slower, whereas hard discs allow fast, direct access to data but are more expensive. Hard discs are usually used to store most of the data, especially data used for interactive processing such as at point of sale and multi-user databases. Magnetic tapes are usually used to make backups of all the data.

Computer crime and fraud

Businesses that employ staff and/or conduct business over the internet can be susceptible to computer crime and fraud. One example would be employees or hackers gaining unauthorised access to financial data and transferring it to an account for their own personal gain. The Computer Misuse Act makes hacking and spreading viruses a criminal offence (for more information on this legislation, see the section on general-purpose packages).

Single entry, multiple use

Data only has to be entered into the system once, and from there it may be used in several different places. Once a company enters details about a new product, examples of multiple use might include: the data may be required by the systems that deal with stock control, ordering, point of sale, advertising, marketing, sales and management information.

Credit question

Two fourth-year pupils are currently on a work-experience placement at their local bank. They are invited to become customers, and their personal details are entered into the system.

a) (i) Will their details need to be entered for each system that requires their information? Explain your answer. {PS 1}

(ii) What kind of database would be required to store their data? {KU 1}

(iii) Data can be accessed randomly or sequentially. Which type of access would be required by the users of the database? {PS 1}

b) The pupils are issued with smart cards but, for security purposes, before the cards can be activated, the pupils have to type in a six-character password.

(i) Suggest two reasons why the bank uses smart cards. {KU 2}

(ii) How could the pupils' passwords be verified? {KU 1}

(iii) Suggest one validation check that could be done to the password. {PS 2}

(iv) Explain the difference between verification and validation. {KU 2}

c) Suggest one example of management information that would be useful to the bank manager. {PS 1}

d) (i) Which piece of legislation covers the security of personal data? {KU 1}

(ii) Who is the data subject and who is the data controller in the bank? {PS 2}

e) One of the services the bank offers to its customers is online banking. Which piece of legislation should help to prevent any concerns that customers may have about fraud? {KU 2}

a) (i) No, the bank can use single entry, multiple use.
   (ii) A multi-user database, so that it can be accessed by several staff members at the same time.
   (iii) Random (direct) access, as the staff will be using interactive processing when dealing with the customers, and this requires fast access to the customers' data.

b) (i) The microprocessor in smart cards cannot be easily forged. Also, data can be updated.
   (ii) The passwords could be entered twice.
   (iii) Length check to make sure that exactly six characters have entered.
   (iv) Verification – data has been entered correctly. Validation – data is sensible. Verification is carried out by humans, whereas validation is carried out by the computer.

c) The busiest days and times of day, so that the manager can employ more staff at these times.

d) (i) Data Protection Act.
   (ii) The data subjects are the customers and the data controller is the bank.

e) Computer Misuse Act.

! Look out for

In previous exams, many candidates had difficulty stating the difference between verification and validation.

Systems software

What you need to know at **General** level ...

- common features of high-level languages
- purpose of high-level languages
- need for translation.

A **high-level language** is a programming language where the instructions are written using everyday English words.

Common features of high-level languages

- Written using everyday English words, making programs quick to write and easy to edit.
- Each high-level language is designed to carry out a specific type of task.
- All high-level languages need to be translated into machine code.
- High-level languages are portable.

Look out for

In previous exams, candidates did not know two common features of a high-level language.

Purpose of high-level languages

High-level languages are designed to carry out specific kinds of task. The types of task include solving mathematical or scientific problems, controlling robots, creating games and building expert systems.

Need for translation

All high-level languages need to be translated into machine code, as machine code is the computer's own language and the only language the processor can understand. Machine code consists of 1s and 0s.

General question

Liam works for a software company, and to date he has written a control program for stationary robots working on a production line, software to run a computerised library system and a program to deal with a large company's accounts.

a) (i) What feature of high-level languages would be useful to Liam in his type of work? {PS 1}

(ii) State two other features of a high-level language. {KU 2}

b) (i) What is needed to turn a high-level language into machine code so that the computer can understand it? {KU 1}

(ii) Is this an example of software or hardware? {KU 1}

a) (i) *Each high-level language is designed to carry out a specific task. Since Liam is writing programs for different types of situation, he is able to select a language appropriate to the task. For example, he might select a control language for programming the robot and a mathematical language for writing the accounts system.*

(ii) *All high-level languages need to be translated into machine code because machine code is the only language the computer can understand. All high-level languages are written using everyday English words, which makes it easier and quicker to write and edit programs.*

b) (i) *A translation program.*

(ii) *Software.*

What you need to know at **Credit** level …

- types of translator:
  - interpreter
  - compiler
- portability of software.

Types of translator

Translators are programs that translate high-level languages into machine code. Two types of translator program are:

1. Interpreter
An interpreter translates one line of code, executes it, then translates the next line of code, executes it and so on.

Advantages

- reports errors immediately
- simple, inexpensive translator program.

Disadvantages

- runs relatively slowly, as each instruction has to be translated every time the program is run
- does not produce an object code, so the HLL program and interpreter must be in RAM while the program is running
- inefficient use of the processor, as it is continually translating code.

2. Compiler
A compiler translates the complete high-level language program and translates it in one go, storing the resultant machine code. The high-level language program is called the **source** code, and the machine code is called the **object** code.

Advantages

- runs relatively quickly once it is error-free, because the object code can be saved and run, therefore the processor does not have to keep translating the source code
- uses up less RAM because the source code and compiler are not required.

Disadvantages

- more expensive, as the compiler is a more complex program than the interpreter
- errors are only reported at the compilation stage.

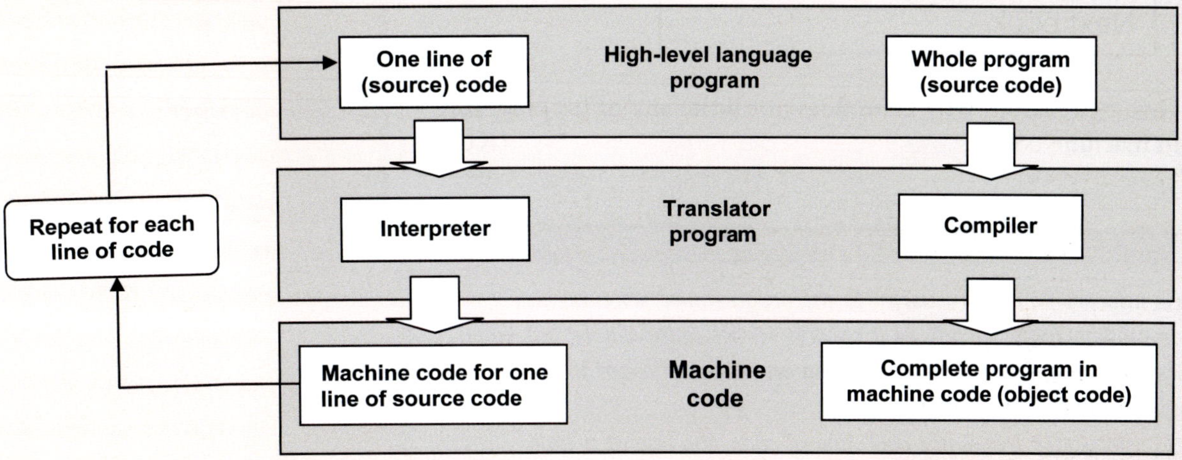

Portability of software

Software is portable if it runs on a computer system or platform other than the one it was written for, with little or no alteration. Software written in a high-level language is usually portable, whereas programs written in machine code only run on the processor they were developed on.

Look out for

Do not confuse portability of **software** and portability of **hardware** – a USB pen drive is an example of a portable backing storage device (hardware) as it is small, light and therefore easy to carry around.

Credit question

a) When Liam is given a new program to write by his employer, his first decision is which high-level language to use. One of the points he takes into consideration is whether or not the high-level language is interpreted and compiled. Explain why this is an important consideration. {KU 1}

b) Explain how both translator programs work, giving advantages and disadvantages of each. {KU 6}

Look out for

In previous exams, many of the candidates did not know about language translation or why a high-level language needed to be translated.

c) The following code is being used to count how many of the 50,000 resources in the library are books. Which translator program would be more efficient at translating the following code? Explain your answer. {PS 2}

```
For book = 1 to 50,000
    If resource type = book then
        Booktotal = booktotal + 1
    End if
Next book
```

d) Give two reasons why Liam does not write any of his programs in machine code. {KU 2}

a) *An interpreter is more useful to the programmer when he is developing the program, as it reports errors immediately; but, when the program is complete, it is faster and more efficient to use a compiled version of the program.*

b) *An interpreter translates each line of code one line at a time. Advantage – errors are reported immediately. Disadvantages include being slow to execute, as the code is translated as it is running; and RAM has to store the high-level language and the translator program while it is executing.*
Compiler takes the high-level language (source code) and translates it in one go into machine code (object code). Advantages – fast to execute, as it is already translated; only the object code has to be held in RAM. Disadvantage – errors are only reported at the compilation stage (after the program has been coded).

c) *A compiler, as it would only have to translate the five lines of code once. The interpreter would have to translate the same five lines of code 50,000 times.*

d) *1. Writing in machine code (a series of 1s and 0s) would be extremely slow, as it would be very difficult to understand and almost impossible to find any errors.*
2. The software would not be portable, as it would only work on the type of computer system it was written for, therefore it could not be sold to anyone who has a different computer system.

Operating systems

What you need to know at **General** level ...

An **operating system** is a set of programs that control the running of the computer and all the devices attached to it.

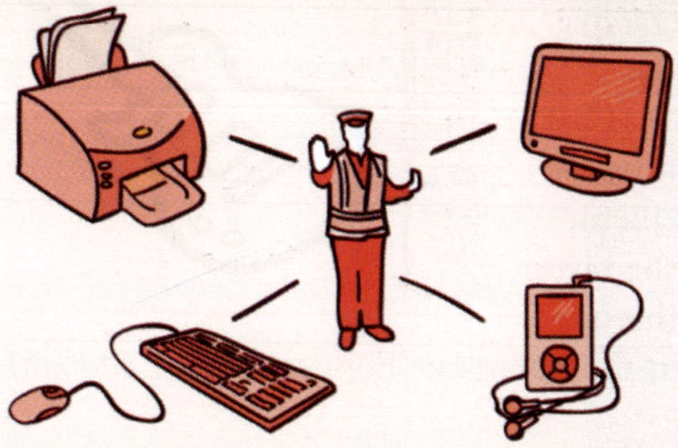

Interactive system

A system where there is a two-way conversation between the user and the operating system.

Real-time system

Real-time systems are used in situations that require an instant response to data input.

Types of file

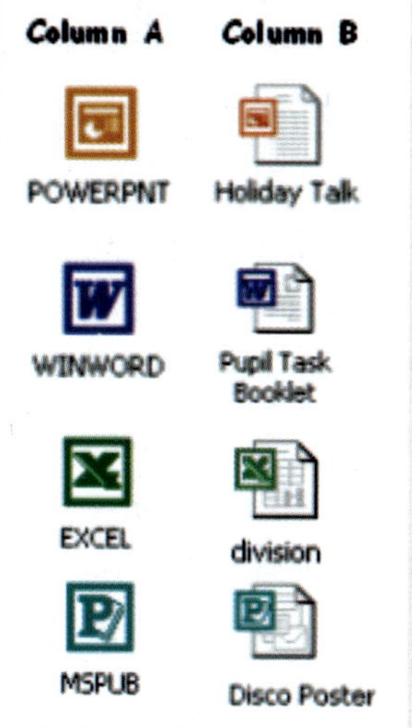

A **program** file is a file that stores a set of instructions that control the processor.

The icons in column A represent applications such as a word-processor (Word) and a spreadsheet (Excel) and are examples of program files.

A **data** file is a file created within a program that holds a user's data.

The icons in column B represent files created by the user, such as the disco poster created in Publisher or the holiday talk presentation created in PowerPoint.

Look out for

A **program** file has in more recent exams been referred to as an **application** file.

Look out for

In previous exams, many candidates did not know the difference between a data file and an application file or entered the definitions the wrong way round.

Ellen is working on a project about guitars for her music assessment.

a) She logs onto the school network and loads up her painting package. Is this an example of an interactive system or a real-time system? {PS 1}

b) Ellen uses the painting package to draw a picture of a guitar which she saves and prints. Using this as an example, explain the difference between a data file and an application file. {PS 2}

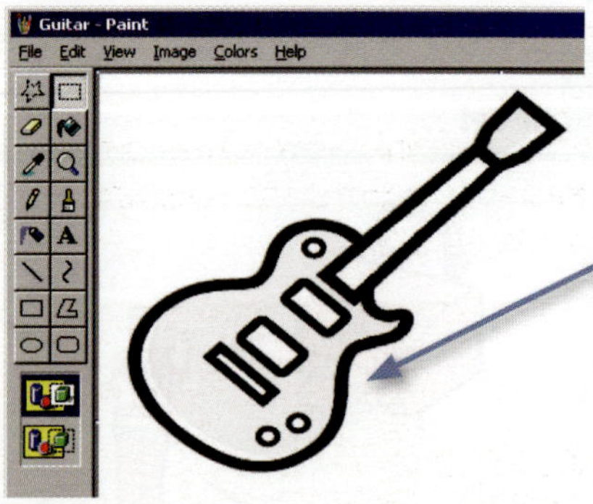

a) An interactive system.

b) The guitar picture she has saved is an example of a data file, and the painting package is an example of an application file.

What you need to know at **Credit** level …

- operating system provides:
  - an HCI for the user
  - file management,
  - memory management
  - error reporting
  - interactive systems with background job capability
  - device drivers
  - hierarchical filing system
  - sequential and direct access to data.

Functions of an operating system

An **HCI** for the user – allows the user to communicate with the computer.

File management – deals with the creation, deletion and amendment of files on backing storage. It also maintains a directory to keep track of information about each file such as filename, file size and where on the backing storage device it is stored.

Memory management – deals with the organisation of currently running programs and data in RAM, making sure that one program or data file does not overwrite another.

Error reporting – the operating system tells the user of any errors that occur.

Interactive systems with background job capability

A background job can be processed whenever the processor is not busy with an interactive job. The interactive job will take priority.

An example would be a computer system at the bank, where the computer deals with requests from customers to withdraw cash (interactive job) and at the same time prints out customers' monthly bank statements to be posted out (background job).

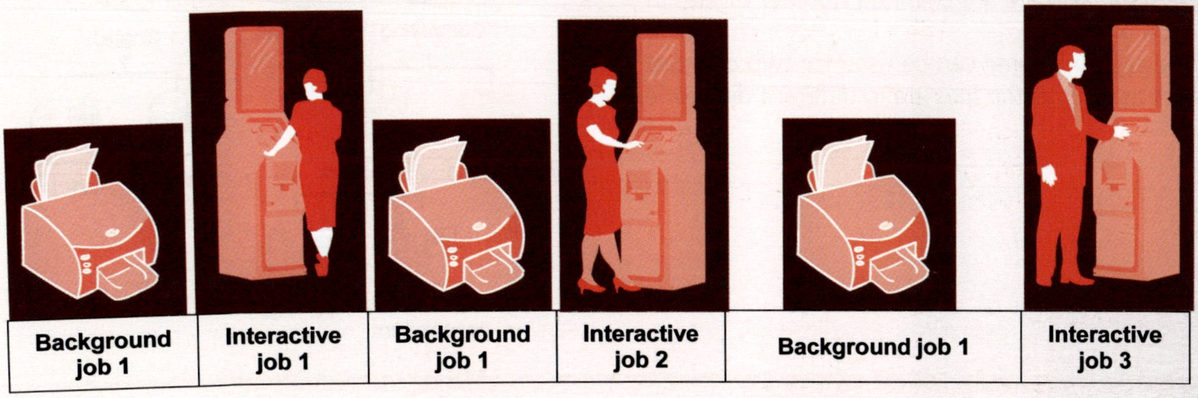

Advantage – in this type of system, the processor is never idle, suspending less important background jobs to accommodate more important interactive jobs.

Device drivers

A device driver is the software that the operating system requires to correctly control the devices attached to the computer. It is possible to attach different makes of printer, mouse, scanner, etc. to a computer because every device has its own device driver software.

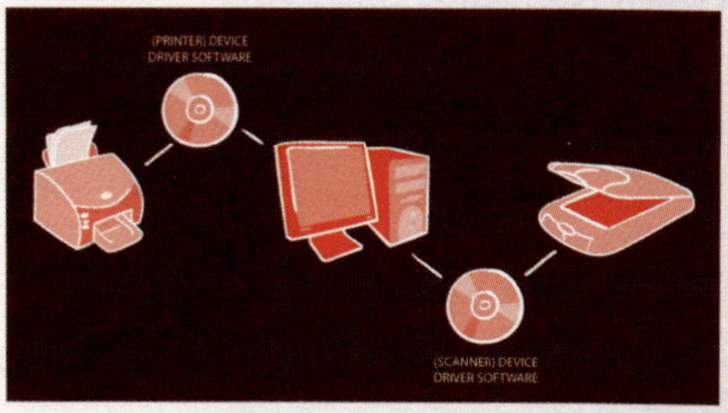

Hierarchical filing system

In order to appreciate the advantages of a hierarchical filing system, let's look at a filing system that does not have a hierarchical structure.

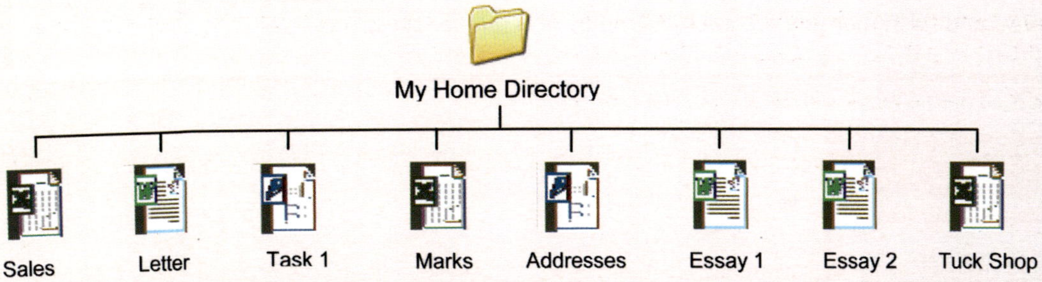

A **hierarchical** filing system contains directories. Each directory can contain subdirectories and or files.

Advantages:

- Files can be grouped together by topic, making it easier for the user to find a particular file.
- When looking in a directory, usually all the files can be seen, as there are a limited number of files in each directory.
- The same filename can be used for two or more files as long as the files are in different directories.

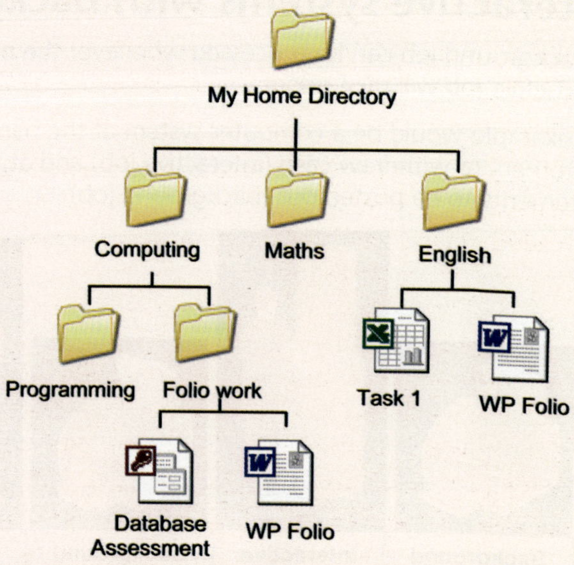

Look out for

A directory is just another word for a folder.

Look out for

When describing advantages, **common mistakes** are:

- quicker for computer to find a file
- takes up less space (storage capacity).

Sequential and direct access to data

Sequential access only allows access to data or a file in the same order as it was saved. This type of access is mainly used for backup purposes. Magnetic tape is an example of a sequential access medium.

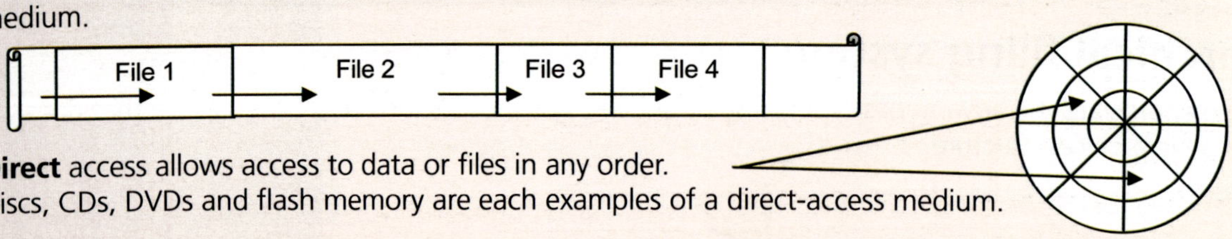

Direct access allows access to data or files in any order.
Discs, CDs, DVDs and flash memory are each examples of a direct-access medium.

Look out for

Random access is another word for **direct** access.

Credit question

Caitlin, the school librarian, switches on her computer and loads up the database that stores information about all the resources in the library.

a) There are two programs running on Caitlin's computer – the database and which other program? {KU 1}

b) Caitlin adds details about two new books that have arrived and re-saves the database.

(i) Will the access to the database be sequential or random? Explain your answer.

(ii) Describe three functions the operating system would carry out while Caitlin is adding the new books. {KU 3}

c) Caitlin wants to print letters to all the pupils with overdue books but needs the computer to be available for issuing books. Explain clearly how both jobs could be done at the same time. {PS 3}

d) (i) A new printer arrives. Caitlin plugs it in and attaches it to the computer – but, when she tries to print, it does not work. Suggest a reason for this. {PS 1}

(ii) Which function of the operating system lets her know that the printer is not working? {KU 1}

e) Caitlin uses a hierarchical filing system so that it is easier for her assistant to find files on the computer. Give two more advantages of using this type of filing system. {KU 2}

a) The operating system.

b) (i) The access will be random, as sequential access requires the computer to search the data in the order it has been stored. This would take too long when Caitlin is issuing books to pupils or when pupils are searching the database for information.

(ii) HCI (human-computer interface) – the HCI allows Caitlin to communicate with the computer so that she can give it instructions about adding data and saving the file.

File management – deals with amending files and updating the directory.

Memory management – this has to keep track of where the currently running programs and data are in RAM.

c) The operating system is interactive, but it has background job capabilities. So, Caitlin could print off the letters using the background capabilities; and, whenever she required to carry out an interactive job, such as issue a book or update the database, the background job would be suspended and the interactive job would take priority.

d) (i) The correct printer driver software has not been installed.

(ii) The error-reporting function.

(iii) The same name can be used for different files as long as they are in different directories and lists of files are not too long, as they are split up according to subject or category.

Look out for

In previous exam answers, the descriptions of functions of an operating system were too vague.

Low-level machine

What you should know at **General** level …

Machine code

Machine code, also known as binary code, contains only 1s and 0s and is the only code the computer can understand; therefore any data entered into the computer has to be translated into the computer's own language before it can be processed.

Representation of positive whole numbers

Positive integers are stored as their direct binary equivalent.

	2^7	2^6	2^5	2^4	2^3	2^2	2^1	2^0
	128	**64**	**32**	**16**	**8**	**4**	**2**	**1**
23 =	0	0	0	1	0	1	1	1
102 =	0	1	1	0	0	1	1	0

Representation of text (ASCII)

All characters that the computer can process have a unique 8-bit code called an ASCII code.

Characters include:

- alphabetic characters (A–Z, a–z)
- the digits 0–9 and
- special characters such as ? , & £ /

Decimal	ASCII code	Character
037	00100101	%
038	00100110	&
048	00110000	0
049	00110001	1
065	01000001	A
066	01000010	B
097	01100001	a
098	01100010	b

Representation of black-and-white bit-mapped graphics

- For a black-and-white image, each pixel on the screen is represented by one bit.
- A pixel is the smallest area on the screen whose colour can be changed.
- The higher the resolution, the more pixels there are per inch.

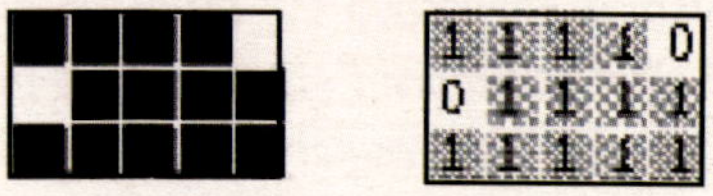

General question

Kevin used his digital camera to take photographs of singers and bands that took part in a recent school concert, and he has since transferred them to his computer.

a) Each photograph is stored as a set of tiny dots. What are these tiny dots called? {KU 1}

b) Explain how the computer stores a black-and-white picture. {KU 2}

c) Kevin has numbered and added a title to each photograph.
   (i) Using the number 54, explain how numbers are stored in a computer. {KU 2}
   (ii) Explain how text is stored in a computer. {KU 1}

a) Pixels

b) Each pixel is represented by a bit (1 for a black pixel, 0 for a white pixel)

c) (i) Numbers are stored as their direct binary equivalent.
54 = 00110110

(ii) Each character has a unique binary code called an ASCII code.

What you need to know at Credit level …

- Calculation of storage requirement of a black-and-white bit-mapped image
- Processor structure:
  - Control unit (CU)
  - Arithmetic and logic unit (ALU)
  - Registers
- Word
- Concept of addressability.

Units of storage

Bit	a single unit in binary (1 or 0)
Byte	made up of 8 bits
Kilobyte	1024 bytes
Megabyte	1024 kilobytes
Gigabyte	1024 megabytes

Calculation of storage requirement of a black-and-white bit-mapped image

1. Calculate the number of pixels in the image. (The number of pixels is equivalent to the number of bits, as each pixel is represented by either a 1 for black or a 0 for white.)
2. Divide the number of bits by 8 to give bytes.
3. Divide the number of bytes by 1024 to give kilobytes (Kb).
4. If appropriate, divide the number of Kb by 1024 to give megabytes (Mb).

! Look out for

Make sure you know your **units of storage**, as you will need these for the calculations of storage requirements for black-and-white images.

Worked example

An image is stored as a black-and-white bit-mapped graphic, measuring 9000 pixels by 7000 pixels.
Calculate the storage requirements in kilobytes.

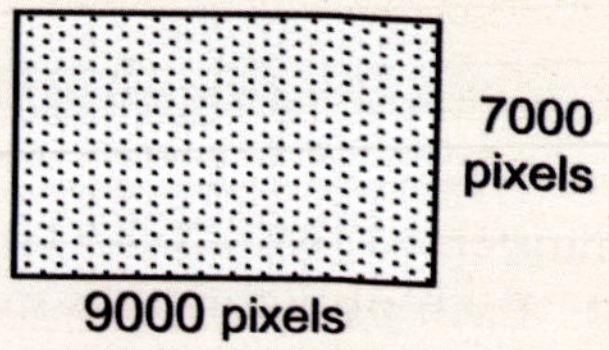

1. 9000 pixels × 7000 pixels = 63 000 000 pixels (= 63 000 000 bits)
2. (÷8) = 7 875 000 bytes
3. (÷1024) = 7690.43 Kb
4. (÷1024) = 7.51Mb

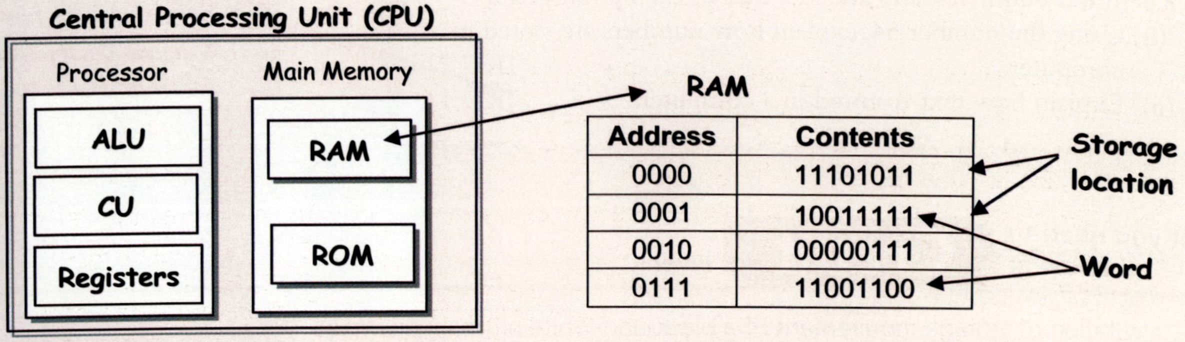

Look out for

In previous exams, few candidates knew that registers were temporary storage locations within the processor.

Processor structure

The processor is made up of three parts:

1. **Arithmetic and logic unit (ALU)** – carries out the calculations and makes the decisions
2. **Control unit (CU)** – controls the running of a program
3. **Registers** – temporary storage locations within the processor.

Look out for

Make sure you **do not** answer 'a Microsoft word-processing package' when asked what a word is.

Main memory

Main memory (RAM) is used to hold currently running programs and data.

Storage location

A place in the computer's memory where an item of data may be held.

Word

A word is the number of bits that can be processed in a single operation. It can store:

- one or more characters
- numbers
- instructions.

Concept of addressability

A way of identifying storage locations in main memory using a unique binary number called an address.

Credit question

At home, Helen loads some coloured photographs from her digital camera into her computer. She then saves them onto her USB flash drive so that she can take them into school to use them in a PowerPoint presentation.

a) (i) Each picture is 1.2 Mb. How many bits are in 1.2 Mb? {PS 3}

b) She has an 8 Gb USB pen drive which has 1.5 Gb of free space. How many pictures can she store? {PS 2}

c) She also scans in an old photograph of herself. The image is stored as a black-and-white bit-mapped graphic, measuring 850 pixels wide by 1200 pixels high. Calculate the storage requirements in kilobytes. (Show all working.) {PS 3}

d) When Helen runs her PowerPoint presentation, the computer loads the data file into memory.

(i) How is each storage location in memory identified? {KU 1}

(ii) What is the term used to describe the number of bits that can be held in each storage location? {KU 1}

e) (i) Which part of the computer's processor is responsible for running a program correctly? {KU 1}

(ii) Which part of the central processing unit carries out calculations and decision-making processes? {KU 1}

(iii) Name two areas within the central processing unit that store data temporarily. {KU 2}

a) 1.2 Mb × 1024 = 1228.8 Kb; 1228.8 × 1024 = 1 258 291.2 bytes; 1 258 291.2 × 8 = 10 066 330 bits

b) 1.5 Gb = (1.5 × 1024) = 1536 Mb ÷ 1.2 Mb = 1,280 pictures

c) 850 × 1200 = 1 020 000 bits = (÷8) 127 500 bytes = (÷1024) 124.51 Kb

d) (i) Each storage location has a unique address

(ii) Word

e) (i) Control unit (CU)

(ii) Arithmetic and logic unit (ALU)

(iii) RAM and registers.

Look out for

When calculating the size of an image: 1 **pixel** = 1 **bit**.

Look out for

Do not confuse the definition of the control unit and the operating system.

Control unit – part of the processor which controls the running of a program.

Operating system – program which controls the operation of the computer, including all the devices attached to it.

Hardware: input, output and backing storage devices

What you need to know at **General** level …

A **computer system** showing data flow:

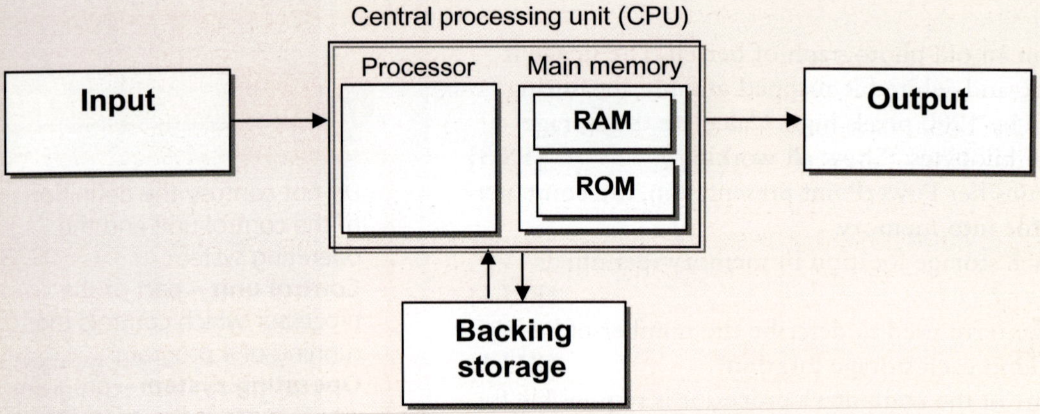

The CPU can be subdivided into the **processor** (the 'brains' of the computer) and **main memory**, with main memory being further subdivided into **RAM** and **ROM**.

RAM – random-access memory

- It holds currently running programs and data
- Its contents are **lost** when the computer is switched off.

ROM – read-only memory

- Can be used to store the start-up program for the operating system
- Can be used to store a program to control a mobile robot (embedded system)
- Its contents are kept when the computer is switched off.

Look out for

Do not confuse RAM with random-access media or random-access devices.

Look out for

See the section on backing storage devices for sequential and random/direct-access devices.

Storage location

RAM and ROM memory is made up of storage locations. Each storage location can contain an item of data.

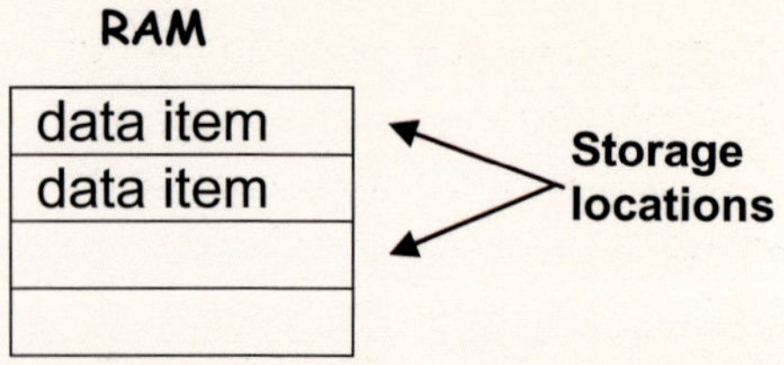

Types of computer

Mainframe

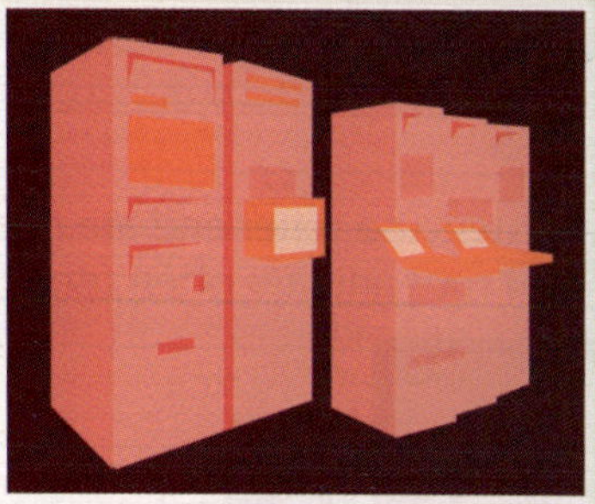

- Very large computer that often takes up a whole room
- Used to process vast quantities of data very quickly
- Input device: **VDU** (computer operator), **terminal** (user)
- Output device – very high-speed printers
- Backing storage – hard disc packs and magnetic tape.

A **desktop** computer is a personal computer used in the home and in the workplace, and is often linked to a local or wide-area network. It cannot be described as easily portable.

A **laptop** computer has similar capabilities to a desktop computer, is portable and is commonly used when travelling or away on business.

A **palmtop** computer usually has a touch-sensitive screen and can fit in your hand or pocket but is not nearly as powerful as other types of computer and is often just used as an electronic diary.

Look out for

This topic is usually linked to questions from commercial data-processing.

Input devices

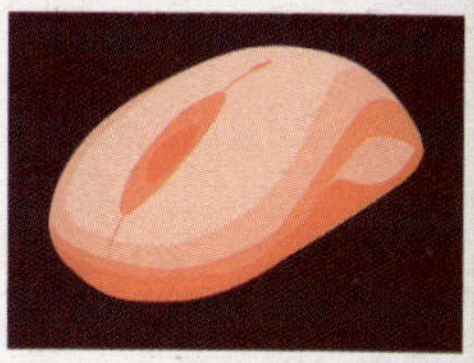

- **Mouse** – usually used on desktop computers and sometimes laptops to move the pointer around the screen and make selections from icons and menus. The older design of mouse used a mouse ball, but computers today use an optical mouse.

- **Trackpad** – usually found on laptop computers to manipulate the pointer in the same way as a mouse.

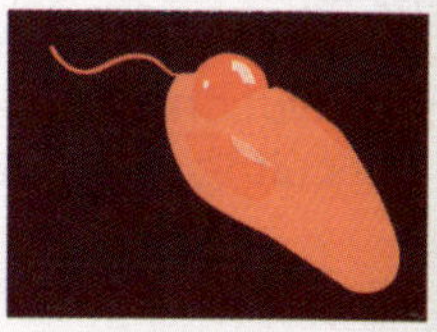

- **Trackball** – similar to an upside-down mouse that uses a mouse ball. Big versions of a trackball can be used with very young children or people with disabilities who have difficulty with motor skills.

- **Scanners** and digital still cameras are able to capture images in digital form so that they can be used in applications such as PowerPoint presentations, web pages, publications, word-processed documents and databases.

- Digital video cameras can capture video and are often used in PowerPoint presentations and web pages.
- Webcam can be used for videoconferencing and creating animations.
- Microphones are used to capture naturally occurring sound.

Output devices
Printers

- **Laser** printers use toner and are good quality, fast and quiet. They are capable of large print runs and are often used in local-area networks.

- **Inkjet** printers are generally cheaper to buy than laser printers, use ink cartridges and produce high-quality colour printouts. They are often used for printing photographs.

Type of printer	Maximum speed (ppm – pages per minute)	Capital (initial) costs	Running costs	Maximum resolution (dpi – dots per inch)
Inkjet	Colour 120 ppm	£30 – £300	Cartridges £10 – £25	1200 × 4800
Laser	Black/white 200 ppm Colour 100 ppm	£100 – £2000	Toner £30 – £200	2400 × 1200

- **Plotters** use coloured pens to produce fine, detailed drawings. They are often used with CAD (computer-aided design) packages.

Look out for

Although it is possible, for example, to buy a very high-specification laser printer that can print up to 200 pages per minute, presently the majority do not print at these speeds. On the other hand, any computing data concerning speed, cost, resolution etc. does not stay the same for very long, so it is difficult to produce an accurate table of information.

Look out for

In previous exams, many pupils did not know what TFT stood for.

Monitors

- **LCD** – liquid crystal display monitors
- **TFT** – thin film transparency monitors have replaced CRT (cathode-ray tube) monitors.

Passive LCDs have poor contrast and slow responses and were used originally with laptop computers. LCD screens nowadays use TFT technology.

- **VDU** – Visual display unit is the term usually associated with a terminal which consists of a screen and a keyboard. Mainframe computers use an operator's VDU so that the operator can enter instructions into the mainframe. Terminals allow users to access a mainframe computer – and, if the terminal is connected via a wide-area network, it is known as a **remote** terminal.

- **Touch-sensitive** screens can be used as an input device. Options displayed on the screen can be selected using a finger or a stylus pen.

Point-of-sale terminal

Computer monitor

Graphics tablet

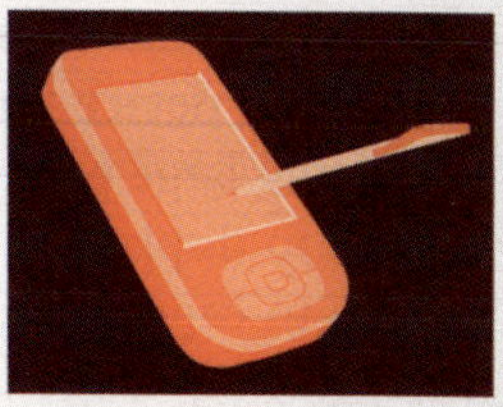
Palmtop/PDA

- **Loudspeakers** come built in with some computers but are not usually of a very high quality. For better-quality sound, speakers can be used, although in a classroom situation headphones would be more appropriate.

Backing storage devices

A **backing storage <u>device</u>** is the hardware, whereas the backing storage **<u>medium</u>** is where the data is actually stored. For example:

CD-ROM drive (device)

CD-ROM (medium)

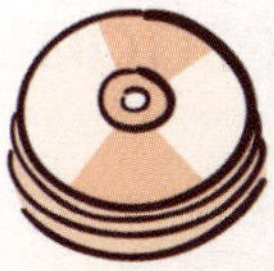

Look out for

A common mistake is to think that a backing storage device is an input device because backing storage devices are used to input the data that is stored on them. Just ask yourself: can this device be used to store data permanently? If the answer is yes, then it is a backing storage device.

Look out for

Many candidates incorrectly use the term 'memory' when they mean 'storage capacity'.

Look out for

Again, it is difficult to produce an accurate table of information, as it is inevitable that magnetic tape, hard discs and USB flash storage will continue to increase in storage capacity.

The table below shows the type of backing storage medium, the relative speeds of the devices and very approximate maximum storage capacities of each medium.

Medium	Speed	Maximum capacity
Magnetic tape	Slow	2 TB
DAT (digital audio tape)	Slow	160 GB (compressed)
Floppy disc	Slow	1.44 Mb
Hard disc	Fast	2 TB
CD-ROM (compact disc – read-only memory)	Medium	700 Mb
CD-R (recordable)	Medium	700 Mb
CD-RW (rewritable)	Medium	700 Mb
DVD-ROM (digital versatile disc)	Medium	17.4 Gb
DVD-R	Medium	8.54 Gb
DVD-RW	Medium	4.7 Gb
Blu-ray	Medium	50 Gb
USB flash	Fairly fast	128 Gb

General question 1

Suggest a suitable device for each phrase:

1. Display computer-aided designs (CAD)
2. An input device for videoconferencing
3. Printing large print runs
4. Used to display information on a desktop
5. Used to capture sound
6. Capture an image digitally
7. Used to output sound
8. Used to display information on laptops
9. Can store moving images
10. Used to make a digital version of a photograph
11. Used to produce a hard copy
12. When your printer at home has run out of ink, you can use it to bring your essay into school to be printed
13. Usually accompanied by OCR software {KU 13}

1. Plotter
2. Webcam
3. Laser printer
4. TFT (thin film transistor)
5. Microphone
6. Digital still camera
7. Speakers
8. LCD (liquid crystal display)
9. Digital video camera
10. Scanner
11. Printer
12. USB flash drive
13. Scanner

General question 2

Suggest an appropriate part of a computer for each phrase:

1. A type of computer often used by business people when travelling
2. The brains of the computer
3. Store currently running programs and data
4. A chip whose contents are not lost when the computer is switched off
5. Used as an electronic diary
6. Processes vast quantities of data very quickly
7. Allows user to communicate with a mainframe. {KU 7}

1. Laptop
2. Processor
3. RAM (random-access memory)
4. ROM (read-only memory)
5. Palmtop
6. Mainframe
7. Terminal or VDU

What you need to know at **Credit** level …

Input and output devices

Below is a table of tasks that require more specialised input and output devices.

Task	Input	Output
CAD (computer-aided design)	Graphics tablet	Plotter
Virtual reality	Data glove	Headset – with earphones and goggles
Disabled user	Braille keyboard, microphone and voice-recognition software, touch talker	Voice output – speech synthesis, magnified screens
Games and multimedia	Joystick Sound card	Sound card, graphics card, speakers
Multimedia presentations	Interactive whiteboard	Multimedia projector
Capture and print an image	Digital camera or scanner	Inkjet printer
Videoconferencing	Webcam and microphone	Screen and speakers

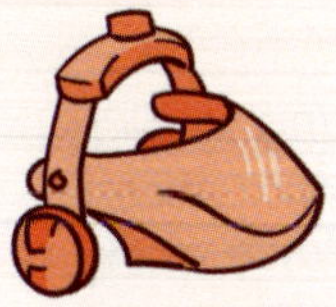
VR headset

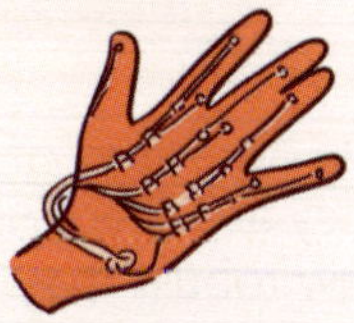
VR data glove

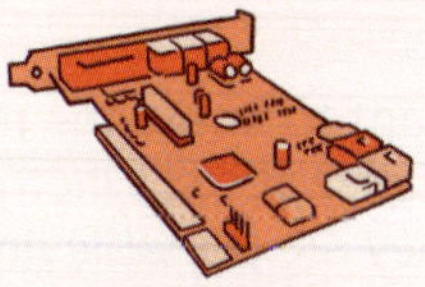
Sound card

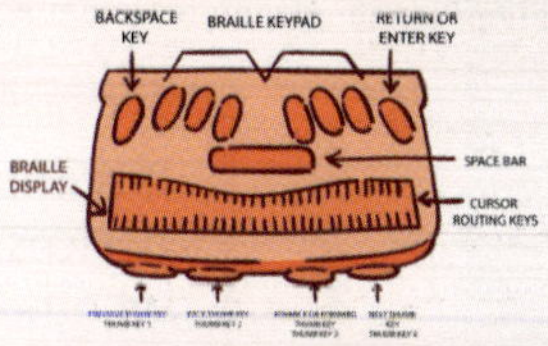

Braille keyboard

Interactive whiteboard

Sound card

- A sound card provides an **interface** for connecting a microphone (input) and speaker (output).
- It has an analogue-to-digital converter to change the naturally occurring **analogue** sound of speech, singing or music into the digital signals processed by the computer.
- It has a digital-to-analogue converter to change the computer's digital signals into the analogue signals required by the speakers.

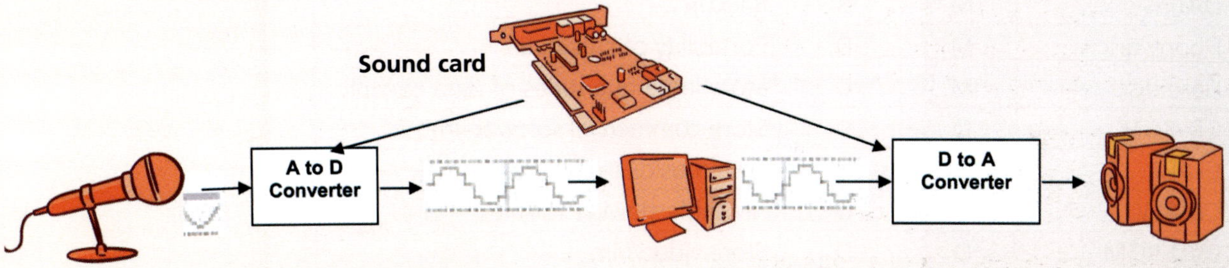

Graphics card

A graphics card is an output device used to enhance the quality of the output to the monitor. It usually has its own RAM and processor in order to free up the central processing unit's resources. This is especially useful for graphics-intensive actions such as playing a fast action game.

Look out for

Sound cards are both input and output devices.

Backing storage

Sequential-access devices mean that files and data can only be read back from the sequential-access medium in the order they were saved.

Magnetic tape devices are the only ones that are sequential access. Tape is slow to access but is cheap and can store vast quantities of data, which makes it suitable for making backup copies. Magnetic tape reels are used with mainframe computers, and one use of DAT (digital audio tapes) is to back up servers on a network.

Direct-access devices allow files and data to be read back in any order. The majority of backing storage devices are direct access and range widely in storage capacity and cost.

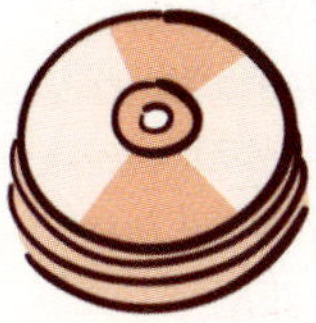

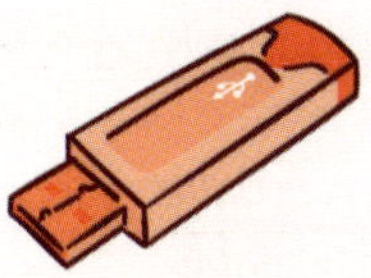

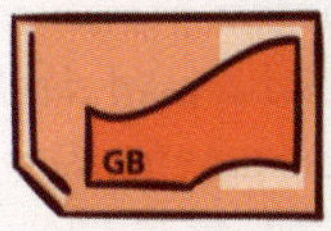

Look out for

Do not confuse backing storage and a backup.

Look out for

It is important to know the relative capacities of backing storage devices, relative costs, whether they are direct or random access, whether they are portable and how robust they are, since many Credit questions give a scenario and you are asked which backing storage device would be most appropriate for the given task.

The table below gives examples of tasks suitable for a particular backing storage device.

Medium	Type	Access	Example of task
Magnetic tape	M	S	Backup
DAT	M	S	Backup
Floppy disc	M	D	Portability of small files
Hard disc	M	D	Store large quantities of data cheaply
CD-ROM	O	D	Store commercial software/music
CD-R	O	D	Save music or data files
CD-RW	O	D	Reusable storage for files
DVD-ROM	O	D	Store video/film
DVD-R	O	D	Save video/music
DVD-RW	O	D	Reusable storage for video etc.
Blu-ray	O	D	Store high-definition film
USB flash	S	D	Portability of files

Type Key: **M** – Magnetic, **O** – Optical, **S** – Solid state
Access Key: **S** – Sequential, **D** – Direct/random

Credit question 1

There are many mnemonics (abbreviations and acronyms) associated with this chapter (hardware; input, output and backing storage devices). Can you give a meaning to each of the following? {KU 20}

1. ppm
2. dpi
3. VDU
4. TFT
5. LCD
6. ADC
7. DAC
8. CD-ROM
9. CD-R
10. CD-RW
11. DVD-ROM
12. DVD-R
13. DVD-RW
14. CPU
15. RAM
16. ROM
17. OCR
18. PDA
19. USB
20. VR

1. *Pages per minute*
2. *Dots per inch*
3. *Visual display unit*
4. *Thin film transistor*
5. *Liquid crystal display*
6. *Analogue-to-digital converter*
7. *Digital-to-analogue converter*
8. *Compact disc read-only memory*
9. *Compact disc recordable*
10. *Compact disc rewritable*
11. *Digital versatile disc read-only memory*
12. *Digital versatile disc recordable*
13. *Digital versatile disc rewritable*
14. *Central processing unit*
15. *Random-access memory*
16. *Read-only memory*
17. *Optical character recognition*
18. *Personal digital assistant*
19. *Universal serial bus*
20. *Virtual reality*

Credit question 2

A word or phrase in each column should link to a word or phrase in the other two columns. Number them accordingly. The first one has been done for you. {KU 5}

A	B	C
1 Flatbed	Laser printer	Visually impaired users
2 Inkjet printer	Sound card	Use less power than a CRT monitor
3 TFT	Drum 1	Plotter 1
4 Sound card	LCD	Are found slotted into the motherboard
5 Speech synthesis	Magnified screen	Both have digital-to-analogue converters
6 Graphics card	Graphics card	Both produce a hard copy

1. Flatbed, drum, plotter
2. Inkjet printer, laser printer, both produce a hard copy
3. TFT, LCD, use less power than a CRT monitor
4. Sound card, graphics card, both have analogue-to-digital converters
5. Speech synthesis, magnified screen, visually impaired users
6. Graphics card, sound card, are found slotted into the motherboard

Credit question 3

For the following tasks, select the most appropriate storage device and state which criteria (access, capacity, cost and portability) are significant and should therefore be taken into consideration. Leave the column blank if the criterion is not particularly important. {PS 4}

1. The sixth-year pupils want to sell an electronic version of their yearbook so that video clips and music from their sixth year events can be included
2. Storing the school library database that pupils can access throughout the day to find resources
3. Making daily backups of the school's file server
4. Taking a copy of your PowerPoint presentation off the school network to do some more work at home.

Task	Device	Direct access	Capacity	Cost	Portable
1	CD-R or DVD-R	√	reasonable	cheap	√
2	Hard disc	√	large		
3	Tape		large	cheap	
4	USB flash drive		reasonable	reasonable	√

Computing in pairs

There are many questions every year which ask you to compare two different words, terms or phrases.

Also, candidates often muddle some words or phrases with other words or phrases.

Below are the most common ones.

First word or phrase	Second word or phrase
analogue	digital
backup	backing storage
barcode information	product info **not** on barcode
bit-mapped graphics	vector graphics
CAD	CAM
CD	DVD
CD-R	CD-RW
check digit	range check
credit cards	debit cards
CRT	LCD / TFT
data	information
data collection and preparation	data input
data type	field type
desktop	mainframe
desktop computer	terminal
device	medium
dial-up	broadband
downloading	uploading
dpi	ppm
field	record
file server	printer server
foreground job	background job
formula	function
freeware	shareware
general-purpose package	integrated package
hacking	viruses
header	footer
high-level language	control language
high-level language	machine code
hyperlink	hotspot
importing data	exporting data
initial costs / capital costs	running costs
interpreter	compiler
LAN	WAN
laser printer	inkjet printer

First word or phrase	Second word or phrase
magnetic guidance system	light guidance system
magnetic stripe cards	smart cards
mail-merge	mailshot
main memory	backing storage
memory management	file management
MICR	OCR
monitor	VDU
multi-access	multi-user
multi-user/multi-access	multi-processor
online	offline
online help	online tutorial
PDA	laptop
portability of software	portability of hardware
program file	data file
programmable robots	intelligent robots
RAM	ROM
real-time processing	interactive processing
relative reference	absolute reference
row	column
scale graphic	crop graphic
search	sort
sequential access	direct access
sequential-access device	random-access device
shareware	commercial
simple formula	complex formula
simple search	complex search
sort ascending	sort descending
source code	object code
spelling-checker	grammar-checker
standard paragraph	standard letter
stationary robots	mobile robots
systems analyst	programmer
template	wizard
text flow	text wrap
text wrap	word wrap
validation	verification

Abbreviations and acronyms

Abbreviations and acronyms are an integral part of computer terminology, and every year there are questions asking what a particular set of letters stands for.

ADC	analogue-to-digital converter
AGV	autonomous guided vehicle
ALU	arithmetic and logic unit
ASCII	American Standard Code for Information Interchange
BIT	**b**inary dig**it**
CAD	computer-aided design
CAM	computer-aided manufacture
CD-R	compact disc recordable
CD-ROM	compact disc read-only memory
CD-RW	compact disc rewriteable
CPU	central processing unit
CRT	cathode-ray tube
CU	control unit
DAC	digital-to-analogue converter
DOS	disc operating system
dpi	dots per inch
DTP	desk-top publishing
DVD-R	digital versatile disc recordable
DVD-ROM	digital versatile disc read-only memory
DVD-RW	digital versatile disc rewriteable
EFT	electronic funds transfer
EFTPOS	electronic funds transfer at point of sale
EPOS	electronic point of sale
Gb	gigabyte
GIF	graphics interchange format
GPP	general-purpose packages
GUI	graphical user interface

HCI	human–computer interface
HR	handwriting recognition
HTML	Hyper-Text Markup Language
IPO	input–process–output
ISP	internet service provider
JPEG	Joint Photographic Expert Group
Kb	kilobyte
LAN	local-area network
LCD	liquid crystal display
Mb	megabyte
MICR	magnetic ink character recognition
NIC	network interface card
OCR	optical character recognition
PDA	personal digital assistant
POS	point of sale
ppm	pages per minute
RAM	random-access memory
ROM	read-only memory
ROV	remotely operated vehicle
RTF	rich text format
Tb	terabyte
TFT	thin film transistor
TXT	text
USB	universal serial bus
VDU	visual display unit
VR	virtual reality
WAN	wide-area network
WIMP	Windows, icons, menus, pointer
WWW	World-Wide Web
WYSIWYG	what you see is what you get

Exam-mark allocation

		GPP	WP	SS	DB	G	DTP	P&M	Web	ES	E COM	LANs	Int	CDP	Aut S	Hard	Inp	Out	BS	Sys S	DS	LLM	
2009 Credit	KU	4	3		4	2				4		2	4	1	8					3	1		36
	PS	6	3	5	5							1	1	2	2		1	2	2	4		2	36
2009 General	KU	4	4	1					1		1	2	2	8	4	5			1	1	2		36
	PS	3	5	7	10	1	1		2		2		1	1	3								36
2008 Credit	KU	3	3	1		1		2				1	4	9	4			1	2		3	2	36
	PS	2	3	5			2	2				1	3	9	2				4		1	2	36
2008 General	KU	2	7	1				1	1			2	3	5	6		2	2		2	1	1	36
	PS		3	9	5	2			2			1	3	4	5				1		1		36
2007 Credit	KU	7	3		1	1			2	2	1	3	4	6	2			2			2		36
	PS	6	1	4	6							3	3	2	3					5		3	36
2007 General	KU		4	3				3		4		2	1	7	2			2	2	3	2	1	36
	PS		1	4	9	2					1			6	7		3	3					36
2006 Credit	KU	3	6	1		1		3			1	3	2	5	5		2			1		3	36
	PS	1	2	4	6	1		2	1		1	4		3	3				3	2		3	36
2006 General	KU		5	1	3				3		3			8	4		2	2		1	2	2	36
	PS	2	2	6	6	1			1	2	3	4	3				1		2	3			36
Total Credit KU		17	15	2	5	5	0	5	2	6	2	9	14	21	19	0	2	3	2	4	6	5	36
Total Credit PS		15	9	18	17	1	2	4	1	0	1	9	7	16	10	0	1	2	9	11	1	10	36
Total Gen. KU		6	20	6	3	0	0	4	5	4	4	6	6	28	16	5	4	6	3	7	7	4	36
Total Gen. PS		5	11	26	30	6	1	0	5	2	3	1	7	15	18	0	4	3	1	2	1	3	36
Total		43	55	52	55	12	3	13	13	12	10	25	34	80	63	5	11	14	15	24	15	22	36

Key for row 1: GPP – General-Purpose Packages, WP – Word-Processing, SS – Spreadsheets, DB – Databases, G – Graphics, DTP – Desk-Top Publishing, P&M – Presentation & Multimedia, Web – Web-Page Creation, ES – Expert Systems, E Com – Electronic Communication, LANs – LANs & WANs, Int – Internet, CDP – Commercial Data-Processing, Aut S – Automated Systems, Hard – Hardware, Inp – Input Devices, Out – Output Devices, BS – Backing Storage Devices, Sys S – Systems Software, OS – Operating Systems. LLM – Low-Level Machine